THE SCHOOL OF
MELCHEZEDEK

Sister Thedra

Copyright © 2021 by Halls of Light, LLC

All rights reserved. This book or any portion thereof may not be reproduced or used in any manner whatsoever without the express written permission of the publisher except for the use of brief quotations in a book review.

ISBN: 978-1-7373071-7-4

To the Reader

Please read and review "Divine Explanations"
on page 188 for questions and definitions of terms.

This book is only a portion of the teachings and
prophecies that have been given by Sananda (Jesus
Christ), Sanat Kumara, and others of the higher realms,
and Recorded by Sister Thedra.

Contents

THE SCHOOL OF MELCHEZEDEK 1

PEACE 67

THE HORRIBLE DAY FOR PAKISTAN 145

Mission Statement 181

Sananda's Appearance 182

About the Late Sister Thedra 183

Divine Explanations 188

Other Books by TNT Publishing 199

Esu Jesus Sananda

This reproduction is from an actual photograph taken on June 1st, 1961, in Chichen Itza, Yucatan, by one of thirty archaeologists working in the area at the time. Sananda appeared in visible, tangible body and permitted His photograph to be taken.

THE SCHOOL OF MELCHEZEDEK

= The Word =

Sori Sori -- Hast it not been said that thy work is not finished? Hast it not been said that greater shall ye do? So shall the Word be fulfilled. So be it and Selah -- Sealed is THE WORD ---

= Truth =

Behold ye in me - the Word - for I am the Word - - I am he which is sent that ye have The Word -- I am he which IS come that ye might KNOW -- So let it be as the Father hast willed

Behold ye in me the Truth - the Way - the Life - the Light which I Am I come that ye might be brot into the realm of Light wherein there is no darkness - no sorrow - no uncertainty ---

= The Traveler =

For the way unto mine place of abode is Light -- While the adepts keep the way - the children of the Father walk within the way - and falter not when the climb is steep - the valleys dark and oppressing --

    They press on - knowing they are not alone - that there is One Who beckons them on - who calls unto them saying: "Fear Not - Fear Not - FEAR NOT - for I am with thee unto the end"

= The Call =

Arise mine children unto the way which I lead thee -- Arise! Arise! Come forth! and ye shall find that thy travels - thy travails have not been in vain - for they are as nought unto thy joys - when thy foot hast been set upon the heights -- And then thou canst see wherein thou hast labored and won the victory -- Then ye shall turn with joy to give a hand unto the one which follows after thee - and ye shall be as an "Elder Brother" unto him - even as I am unto thee --

I say: "Fear Not!" for I have gone before thee that ye might find thy way -- And be ye not deceived - - I too - have walked the same path that ye now tread - -

I too - have prepared mineself for the victory won - -

I too - have walked the valleys and the steeps - - the crags I have scaled - the rocks have bruised mine body - the darts have pierced deep within mine body - - and yet - I won the victory over flesh -- The spirit prevailed over death - and I now stand upon the High Holy Mount as one prepared to assist thee in thy flight ---

= **The Master** =

I say - I am prepared to assist them in thy flight -- And ye too - shall be as the Victor - and ye too shall praise the name of Solen Aum Solen as I -- Ye too - shall know Him as I know Him - - and be ye as one prepared even as I - - for this I say unto thee in His Name - that His Will be done So let it be ---

(Come ye at another hour - and be ye blest for thy coming)

= **Loyalty** =

This is mine word unto thee - and it behooves about the Father's business - even as I -- And at no time shall ye betray thyself - at no time shall ye turn from thy appointed course -- At no time shall ye betray thine trust -- At no time shall ye deny me - The Lord thy God - - for it is I - that hast prepared the way before thee -- So be it that I am with thee that ye might be prepared to enter into mine place of abode ---

= Watchfulness =

There are many called - - few are prepared - yet it is said: "Be ye alert and watchful - that thy foot slips not"-- Watch! be ye alert and be ye as one prepared to do battle with the forces of DARKNESS - for they sleep not - neither do they give* - - without mercy they willed the sword, the sword of death - and at no time do they show mercy ---

(*retreat - weaken)

= The School of Melchezedek =

Sori Sori -- For this Word hast thou prepared thyself - and it is for the good of all that I give unto thee this part - - it shall be called: "The School of Melchezedek"- and this shall be the School of the Initiates - Not one shall enter without the proper preparation -- The preparation is that which is the "Passport" which entitles them to pass thru the portals of the School of Melchezedek --

Not one passes without the proper preparation --

It is thy part to give unto them as ye have been given to - As ye have received - so shall ye give unto them -- Their part is to receive that which is proffered -- None shall be forced - none shall be brot unprepared - neither shall preference be shown ---

= Service =

No price is placed upon their head - no price is placed upon them - - their puny penny is of no value within the School of Melchezedek - for it is earned by labor - and service to mankind - without thought of self SELFLESS service -- And no man enters herein without the qualifications - without his record which follows him where he goes - it also precedes him - for it cannot be hidden from him - neither from the Mighty Council ---

= T-M-C =

The Mighty Council admits him and prepares for the next step - his work - and for his part - his welfare - - and he has but to apply himself diligently - whole heartedly - and without thought of self ---

= Protection =

For this do I say unto thee: "Let thy foot not slip - let thy hand be mine thy words mine - - let it be that I am thy Shield and thy Buckler" ---

= Obedience =

For this do I say: "Come - follow ye me - and I shall bring thee safely". So be it and Selah ---

= For the Record =

Write ye that which I give unto thee to write - and it shall serve its purpose - - it shall not be lost to the ravages of TIME - for I shall see to that - for every word that hast been written is recorded on solid - pure golden leaves - which are placed within the secret place wherein no mortal hand might destroy --

Put thine hand in mine and I shall lead thee thru the archives of time wherein such things are to be seen and understood - wherein there is no waste or erosion --

Better shall ye understand when ye have seen these records - - better shall ye prepare thyself for thy next part ---

= Admonition =

Now ye shall do that which I give unto thee to do - and ye shall not quibble over words - neither shall ye be as one which is lacking in knowledge - - for have I not brot thee hence? Have I not given unto thee strength - and the authority to speak for me - in mine name?

Now ye shall do the things I give unto thee to do - and ye shall not fail --

Be ye as one prepared - - walk ye with surety - and ask favors of no man -- Be ye as one on whose head I place mine hand - and in whose hand thine hand rests --

Wait upon me - and serve the Light which I Am ---

= Love =

My Word is valid - and I am come that ye might have Light - that darkness be dispelled -- And at this time I would say unto thee: The way is open unto them which have the will to follow me -- There is but one way unto mine Father's place of abode - - that is Truth - and Justice which brings the other aspects -- Wherein have they been enumerated wherein have they been pointed out?

Yet I say unto the one which would follow me: Love is the secret - Love manifests itself in Truth and Justice - Mercy - and Charity --

Fail ye not in this - -

And for it is the first attribute of Love -- These attributes are but part of the One Whole of the Father - the fulfilling of the Law --

The fulfillment of the Law is LOVE - -

And for this does the Father send me - that ye might know the meaning of Love -- For this have I touched thee - - for this hast thine own heart been cleaven - - and for this hast thou sorrowed for the fallen of mankind - for the sunken - and depraved ---

= Responsibility =

Bless those which sorrow for them - for they shall be lifted up --

Yet I say: Ye shall not be as an ass unto them - for they shall not ride upon thy back --

They shall carry their own burdens - and make ready themself for to receive their own passport - their own inheritance --

So let them learn the way of the Initiate - the way of righteousness and all shall be well with them ---

= Victory =

This I would point out unto thee: There is one which would put within thy hand the sword of Truth - and the power to wield it - - yet that One <u>ever</u> knows his part - his responsibility unto himself and his station - his office -- He hast won his victory thru and by obedience unto the Law - unto the Brotherhood of the Melchezedeks ---

= The Sacrifice =

I say - this loyalty is the outcome of long training - long long experiences - which causes the candidate to bring himself unto the Altar of the Most High Living God as a <u>living</u> <u>Sacrifice</u> ---

= The Guardian =

Therein he begins his preparation for his Adeptship - his Sonship --

He cries out for Light - that he might serve the Light - that all men might be lifted up -- And he then is heard - found - and given as it is wise and prudent -- He fares well - for as he is prepared he receives - and none are overlooked --

For the candidate is never alone - he is accompanied by one which has been assigned unto him for the purpose of prompting him in the time of doubt - and in the time of trial -- While he walks in silence for the most part - he is present - and for that matter he is watchful - for the enemy draws nigh unto the candidate when the victory is most won ---

= Free Spirit =

I say unto thee: Be ye mindful of thy "Guardian" and let him be unto thee thy Shield and Buckler - - for this does he walk with thee - and ye shall be as one blest to be aware of him - for he cares for thee in the hours of thy unknowing - in the hours of thy sleep -- Yet it is said - ye sleep not - for thy body of flesh sleepeth - while thy "Am" returneth unto the place of instruction - that ye be filled with knowledge and wisdom ---

= The Melchezedeks =

The School of Melchezedek is the place wherein ye are trained -- The Melchezedeks are the Ones which are trained - which have been trained for their part - - for their places differ one from the other - and yet all are part of the GREAT and DIVINE PLAN - the plan which was before the world WAS! So be it that the Melchezedeks are the Ones which are prepared to bring order out of chaos - and it shall be the Order which shall not be broken - the Order which shall be perfect - and the Order which shall withstand the destruction of man --

The destruction of man shall be as nought - for it shall be as a foul wind which shall pass before a gentle breeze -- So be it - it is decreed and prophesied aforehand -- So let it be as The Father hast willed it ---

= Each unto His Part =

Wherein is it said that ye shall walk with me and talk with me -- it shall be according unto the plan - And not one shall be out of his place - not one shall be unaccounted for - for all the ones which have heard mine voice and answered me shall be as ones of mine fold - for I shall gather them in as part of the fold -- And these shall be as none other - for they shall be as ones set apart for that which they are to do - and they shall be trained in that part - and none shall trespass upon the part of the other each shall have his own part - and all parts shall fit into the Great Whole the One - - for not one shall do the work of another - each shall do his own work and know that which he is to do --

Be ye as one prepared - - for this do I call unto thee this day - that ye might come forth - - and be ye free from all bondage - from all darkness --

Know ye the true from the false - - seek ye the Truth and no harm can befall thee --

Bless thyself - as none other can bless thee - for it is given unto thee this day to choose thy way - the way ye shall go - and no man shall say unto thee nay!

= Offspring =

Prepare thy household that it might be in order - let thine offspring be as ones prepared that they might choose wisely -- And be ye as one responsible for the training of thy offspring - that they know the true from the false --

Pay ye no heed to the promptings of man's opinions -- Seek ye the Light - and walk ye in It fearlessly - for I have prepared before thee the Way - and ye have but to seek and ye shall find - for it is the law ---

= The Light =

Born of the Light art thou - born of TRUTH art thou - and ye shall come to know thy Source -- So be it The Father's Will --

Let it be known that I Am come that ye be blest - that ye be lifted up --

Let it be known that I am in the place wherein there is no darkness for the Light expels the darkness - - for the Light expands and the darkness decreases into nothing --

This is the Word I give unto them which seek the Light: The Light increases according to thy capacity to receive it - for thou art as yet not come into the fullness of thy inheritance - - thy capacity is not sufficient as yet -- For this I come that thy capacity be increased - for this hast the School of Melchezedek been established upon the Earth -- For this hast ones been sent that there be Light in the Earth ---

Never hast there been so great a stir as this day - when so many run hither and yon - seeking the way of salvation -- They know not from whence they come - neither where they goeth --

When it comes that they are called unto their places which they have prepared themself for - they shall find that they have not understood the Way of "The Lord" - they have been blinded by man's opinions and man's offal --

There are ones which have taught the teachings of the Ancients – and thot them truth - yet unto these I would say: Great hast been the changes made since the beginning of these Great and Good things which were given for their time and age - for they served well their time and peoples -

Yet - now that which was set forth in All the Great works given for man's upliftment/ enlightenment - is safeguarded - and held in trust for them which seek Truth and Light --

While the Key lies within thy hand - it is concealed from the unprepared - the eyes of the unjust and imprudent - that they might not find and misuse it for their own end --

Therefore I say unto thee: Be ye as wise - and give not thy pearls of great price unto them which would tear down and destroy --

I say: "Tear down - and destroy" for there are ones which do wear the sacred symbols - and the robes of color - that they be noticed - heard seen - and praised for their goodness and humility --

I say! Beware lest thy foot slips - for thy authority comes not thru the outer display of colors - signs and amulets ---

$$= \text{Evil} =$$

Listen while I tell thee of the Sorcerer's lot - Be ye as one mindful of him which sits in wait for his prey - - as the vulture he sits with bated breath - that he might bring into his lair the prey - and use him unto his own vicious end -- I say - beware the sorcerer and his partners - for they do bear witness of each other - they bear the same mark - that of the beast --

Behold ye the mark - and wait upon me that ye fall not prey unto his wiles and schemes --

Hast it not been said - that the Victor is the Victor - for his strength hast overcome the evil of the enemy - - it is so -- By his own effort shall he overcome all evil - - by his own strength shall he overcome the evils which confront him - and which shall be put in his way --

Therefore I say unto thee: Fear not - for I am come that ye have the path clearly marked - - all the pitfalls are clearly marked - - all the parts which have confronted thee shall be made clearly - and ye shall arise with honor and dignity -- So be it and Selah ---

= **It is Lawful** =

Wherein is it said that: "When the student is ready the Master will appear"?

Hast it not been said: "As ye are prepared so shall ye receive"? It is lawful that I say unto thee: I am come <u>this day</u> that all might have Light It is lawful that I say - that I Am come that they which are of a mind to follow me might be brot out of darkness --

Yet it is not lawful that I give unto the uninitiated that which they have not prepared themself for to receive -- This I too would say: That when thou hast prepared thyself for to receive me - I shall make mine self known unto thee - - and for this have I come into the Earth - that I find mine own - and that they might come to know me even as I know them -- So shall it be that <u>these</u> shall go where I go - and they shall be as ones prepared to do that which I do - for they shall be mine own - and they shall wear the Crown which shall be firmly placed upon their head by The Most High - and He shall bless them as none other - for He shall endow them with the power which shall be theirs to keep - - for by their own effort - obedience - and loyalty shall they prove themself TRUSTWORTH --

I am come this day that this might be so -- So be it that I have offered unto <u>All</u> mine hand - mine love - mine assistance -- I have said: "Come - Come follow me "- and unto all which come I say: Be ye as ones trustworth - as ones prepared to go where I go -- Falter not - turn not thy face from me - for I shall do that which I have said I shall do - I shall not fail thee - I shall do mine part - - for this am I sent that ye be lifted up - even as I --

Let it be understood that none enter into the place wherein I abide unprepared - - <u>none</u> come unprepared! for I am the Gate Keeper - I am the Porter at the Gate - and none enter unaware --

I bring them which are prepared to enter herein -- I bring them even before the Throne of the Most High - and before Him - they bow unto Him in holy adoration and with praise for - unto - the Great and Grand Majesty of His Being---

= The Holy Rites =

They are as ones which have earned the Rites - they have been found worthy to partake of the Holy Rites of Initiation - wherein they shall be prepared to do Greater things --

They shall be blest to go where I go - and do the things I do - and they shall be as the Sons of God by Divine Rite - and no man shall take from them the power and authority to do His Will -- Therefore I say unto thee: Behold ye the Glory of The Lord thy God - and be ye as one prepared to go where He leads thee -- Fear not - for He is Sent of The Most High - Who is The Father of All - The Source of thy Being - for in Him thou art - - thou art of Him begotten

For this hast He sent me - that ye might return with me - even as ye went out --

Be ye mindful of thy Source - and fear nought - for He is thy Shield and thy Buckler ---

= Gratitude =

Praise ye the Name of Solen Aum Solen - - -

Sori Sori -- I say unto thee: This shall be the handbook for them which are ready to receive this mine Word - and they shall be as ones blest to receive it - - they shall be as ones prepared to receive yet Greater Light and knowledge -- Now ye shall withhold this part from them which have not had the preparation to receive - - the ones which have fallen by the way shall not be given this part - for it is not for them --

I say unto them which receive this part: Be ye as one responsible for that which ye do with it - for it is part of thy preparation for Greater responsibility -- Be ye as wise as the serpent and silent as the Sphinx.

Recorded by Sister Thedra

Councils - Schools - Brotherhood

Sori Sori -- For this time let it be done as the Father would have it be - It is given unto me to come as one Sent -- and for this have I come as one Sent -- Now ye shall put on the whole Armor of God - and ye shall be as one prepared for the part which shall be given unto thee -- Ye shall be as one which shall walk tall - and ye shall not fail - neither shall ye want -- Be ye as one blest to receive me - and ye shall be as one in whose favor I shall be - - be ye blest this day -- Accept that which I give unto thee in the name of the Father Mother Son - for it is of Him that I am Sent---

Ye shall accept this mine word - and ye shall give it unto them which await it - in the name of Our Father - Solen Aum Solen - - for this is mine word on which ye might rely - for it is valid -- Give unto me credit for knowing that which I say unto thee - for I am one of the School of Melchezedek - I am one of the Brotherhood of Melchezedek yet ye distinguish not the difference -- I say All are one under the Mighty Council - the OVER ALL Council -- Wherein is it said that the Mighty Council is the High Council under which ALL other councils function ---

Some are lesser than others - yet all who serve as the servants of the Most High are in the care and direction of the Great and Mighty Council - each having its head - each having its part within the whole - while none exist separate - and without guidance in some measure -- The Great and Mighty Council is the Source of the Light which is focused unto the lesser councils - as they are prepared to receive - each as he is capable of receiving ---

There are ones which stand with their hands before their eyes - fingers in their ears - that they hear not - nor see that which is done by these Councils of Light -- Therefore they receive lesser light - wisdom understanding - wherefore it is said: Take thine fingers out thine ears and hear that which is said - for the time is come when great Light shall be given unto the one which seeks the Light

For this do I say unto thee: Pay ye heed to that which is said - - it is said in such a manner that the uninitiated might not read the meaning thereof - that he might not see that which is hidden from the uninitiated the eyes of the profane - - I say it is hidden up from the unjust ---

They shall not see - they shall not find that which is hidden - for they would but misuse that which is revealed unto the "Initiate"---

Pay ye heed - and listen - see - and know ye that which is hidden - for this is it said: "Seek the Light - see the Light - walk ye in it" ---

Place thine own self on the altar of the Most High Living God - as a living sacrifice - - Behold ye the glory of such sacrifice - for ye shall find therein thy own self--

Behold ye all things made new -

Behold ye the Glory of God -

Behold ye the Glory of the Heaven -

Behold ye the Being which thou art -

Behold ye Me - the Light which I Am -

Behold ye the Source of Light -

For the Father Mother hast sent thee forth as part of the One -- In Him thou art staid - in Him thou hast thy being -- So be it and Selah --

Recorded by Sister Thedra

Assurance

Sori Sori -- This mine word I would give unto them which have received "The Hand Book of The Melchezedeks"- and it is for their own good that I give unto them this mine word - - for it shall be as a reminder unto them of the responsibility which goes with such as they have sought (the Knowledge of the Initiate) - the Power of the Initiate I say it is great - and for this hast it been said: "Prepare thyself for to receive"- - for this is it said: "Be ye as one trust worth"---

Now it is come when one shall try to disarm thee - when thy trials shall be as never before - and when thy friends shall forsake thee - and when thy families shall be as thy enemies - and thy strength shall avail thee nought

It is then that ye shall cry out for assistance/ for help/ for the strength which hast failed thee --

Yet I say unto thee: FEAR NOT! for thou art not alone - thou art NOT alone! For that matter there is a Mighty Host ready to assist thee Be ye as one prepared to accept that which they proffer -- So be it and Selah ---

I bring unto thee assurance that I am with thee unto the end -- So be it that I shall not forsake thee in the time of thy trials and temptation.

Be ye aware of Them - know ye that there is the Host - and one which walks by thy side - ever ready to assist - when it is wise and expedient ---

I say unto thee - be ye as one prepared - and ye shall prove thyself <u>trustworth</u>!

So be it as the Father hast willed it --

T. = Remember Jesus' initiations - -

Recommended references:- Bible - Aquarian Gospel Vale Owens' Lowlands of Heaven - Highlands of Heaven -Ministry of Heaven - Battalions of Heaven --

Recorded by Sister Thedra

Sonea - One of the Host

Sori Sori -- Long hast it been since I have spoken - yet the time is come that I shall again speak unto thee - - for it is the will of mine Father Solen Aum Solen -- For this I speak - - for this do I say unto thee: Ye shall be as one blest to receive me - and that which I have for thee -- It is for the good of all that I come this day - and it behooves me to say unto thee - that mine word is valid - and ye shall bear witness of me - and mine word ---

Let it be known that there is a Host of Mighty Enlightened Ones which serve thee - which serve the Father - for He is the Light - the Truth - the Way - and there is no other -- We of the Host bear witness of Him - for We are His Hands and feet made manifest unto thee ---

We - of the Host - have given of Ourself that ye might know - that ye might be brot out of bondage - that ye might have Light - that ye might be one of "The Host"-- So be it as The Father hast willed it ---

I come as thy Sibor - known as Sonea - as One which hast kept an eye on thy progress - and one which hast kept thee in the time of unknowing -- So be it that I am with thee - and I shall be unto thee an Elder Brother - and ye shall be as the younger brother - - for this shall I go before thee and lead the way - and no harm shall befall thee -- Ye shall walk in places strange - and far - yet I say - no harm shall befall thee --

= The Very Small Seed =

Come - Come - let us explore regions far and strange - without fear or anxiety -- There are regions strange and far - unexplored by thee - which need thee and thy assistance ---

There are ones yet unborn in flesh of Earth - which await the coming into Earth -- These are of the <u>new</u> generations unborn - which shall be given the assistance necessary for their coming -- These shall find a new world strange unto thee - yet the two shall be integrated as one - for this New Generation shall have their memory in part - - therefore they shall be better prepared for their <u>new part</u> -- Let it be known that these things shall be done in the New Day - - The day is now come when ye shall know that all is one - - yet I say unto thee: "In mine Father's House are many Mansions" - it is true - and ye shall come to know as I know - - for thy world shall become as a Very Small Seed in the Granary of mine Father's Kingdom - - for He hast places far - and near - which thou knowest not - - far - and near - I say! for thou hast not even explored the fullness of the world at thy feet - neither above thy head -yet I say unto thee: Come - and I shall take thee farther out - where there is no darkness - no confusion - no lethargy - no sorrow - without fear - and without haste -- Come - Come and I shall lead thee - be ye as one forewarned - forearmed - foreprepared ---

Let it serve thee well - for I am He which stands by thee in the hours of thy unknowing ---

I Am He - - I AM HE - which is Sent --

So be it as The Father hast Willed it --

Recorded by Sister Thedra

Sori Sori -- For this have I called thee at this hour - that ye might add this unto that which hast been given unto thee for them which are prepared to receive -- So let it be for the good of all --

= Initiation =

This I would say that they might know - that they might be blest to know ---

There is a time of unknowing - and a time of knowing -- The time of knowing is now come - when there shall be ones prepared to receive certain truth - - certain truth which is wise to unveil at THIS time ---

There is a time to unveil certain truth - portions at a time - unto certain ones which are prepared to receive it ---

These have been called "Initiates" -- These have been initiated into the so-called "Mysteries" - and these are prepared to receive these <u>unrevealed</u> truths - that is - that which hast been veiled from the uninitiated ---

= Mysteries =

These things are no longer a mystery when revealed - - for thy unknowing - are they mysteries --

These so-called mysteries are that which is truth and law - that which operates by natural law - - and when understood there is no mystery --

This I would point out unto the ones which ask for light:--

Be ye as ones trustworth - as ones prepared to receive - for great responsibility goes with knowledge – Great responsibility goes with Gifts which are given of the Spirit

Now for this I would say unto them which ask for Gifts: Be ye aware of the responsibility which accompanies such Gifts --

For this is it said: "Prepare thyself" - "Be ye trustworth" - "Betray not thy trust - thyself" - "Put thy foot not into a hole" --

= For This =

For this is one sent that ye be aware of thy responsibility--

For this is one sent that ye be prepared --

For this is one sent that ye might not fall - neither shall ye fear --

For this is he thy constant companion --

For this is it said: "When the student is ready the Master will appear"-- It is So -- So be it and Selah ---

Now - I would say unto thee: Be ye sure of thy footing - - let thy feet be firmly planted -- Let thy speech be the speech of the Initiate -- Let thy hand be firmly planted in His - the One Sent - and ye shall be as one led firmly and gently - unto heights undreamed of ---

Let it be known that there are greater heights - greater attainment - greater responsibility – greater revelations - Greater Glories ---

Behold ye the Glory of the Heights!

For this have I come - that ye might attain the Heights

Recorded by Sister Thedra

Sponsors

Sori Sori--

Be it expedient that I say unto thee this day - that the way is made clear before thee - and it behooves thee to go before them - as I have gone before thee - for they shall be as the younger brothers which are to follow --

I say they - the younger brothers which shall follow thee shall be as the "porters at the gate" for the ones which are yet unborn --

They shall stand sponsor for the ones to follow after them -- It is the law: As one is "raised up" he gives assistance unto them which come after them - - Therefore it is said: "Be ye as one prepared for that which ye are to do"--

Give unto me thine hand - and I shall put into it a plan - and it shall serve thee well - and ye shall not fail --

Be ye faithful unto thy trust - betray not thyself - and give unto me credit for knowing that which I say unto thee -- Fear not - hold ye steadfast - - Give unto the Source of thy Being credit for thy Being - - praise ye the name of Solen Aum Solen --

Harken unto mine voice - and be ye as one responsible for that which is given unto thee to do -- Wear ye the Royal Robe with dignity and with power - the power which is endowed unto thee of the Father Mother God - and ye shall be as a Son of God --

Let thine light so shine that others might know that ye are as a Son which hast the Seal upon thy forehead - for they shall see it - and they shall be as ones which find thee - - by thy own light shall they be drawn unto thee -- They shall be as the ones seeking Light - and ye shall give unto them assistance - even as I assist thee --

Be ye as the forerunner of me - for ye shall prepare them to receive me - - for is it not said: "Ye go before me to prepare the way for my coming"--

I have gone before thee that ye might find thy way back unto thy Source - - now ye are to prepare them that they might receive me - even as thou hast received me - - and they shall come to know me even as ye know me -- So be it and Selah --

Recorded by Sister Thedra

The Covenant

Sori Sori -- For this hour let this be done according unto mine Father's Will - and it shall be for the good of all mankind -- So let it be -- Amen and Selah --

Be ye as one which hast the will to do that which shall be given unto thee to do - and ye shall not want - neither shall ye fail --

This I would say unto thee: Be ye as one prepared to go forth as a bride adorned to meet her bridegroom - for he cometh - and he approaches swiftly - and surely --

The bridegroom cometh as "One Sent"- and ye shall accept him as One Sent of the Father - for such he is - - and he shall claim thee as His Own - and no man shall say unto Him - nay!

Be ye as one blest to receive Him - for he is the Son of the Most High Living God --

Blest shall ye be - for he shall take thee as a bride which is prepared to receive her bridegroom --

Blest shall ye be - for ye shall abide with him as one wed unto him and ye shall not be found wanting --

While it is said - thy work hast but begun - I say: Greater things shall ye do - for ye shall walk knowingly - ye shall be as one on whose shoulders I place mine mantle - and I shall give unto thee a plan which shall be the Covenant twixt them and me - and no man shall turn thee aside - neither shall he deter thee from thy course --

Be ye as one which hast covenanted with me - - remember thy covenant - made so long ago - - for this shall be revealed unto thee - - for this do I say: "Remember"- for this I say: "Be as one prepared"--

By thine own hand shall I lead thee -- By thine own will shall ye follow where I lead thee -- By thine own light shall thy way be made smooth --

Sori Sori -- For this hour I say hear ye me - - And know ye that I am He which is come - that ye be brot out of bondage -- For this have I quickened thee - and it shall be for the good of All - that I bring thee forth - that they too might be quickened --

Let them which have <u>ears</u> hear that which I say unto thee - for it shall profit them --

Withhold not this mine word from them - for it shall be as mine word unto them - that they might know me - even as ye know me -- So be it as the Father hast willed --

Bear ye witness of me - carry high mine banner - bear ye the name which I have given unto thee - - let all men adore the name which I have given unto thee mine own --

Retreat not - for I say: The dragon shall approach thee as one which has the power to attack - - yet he shall not overcome thee - for I am with thee unto the end --

Be ye not fearful - for I shall be thy Shield and thy Buckler - - I shall not forsake thee in thy hour of trial --

Hast it not been said: "I Am thy Shield and thy Buckler"- I Am He which stands porter at the gate - that no evil befall thee -- I AM HE - Sent - that ye might not fail -- So be it and Selah --

Recorded by Sister Thedra

Sori Sori -- So be it that there is one which hast his hand upon thee - and he hast come unto thee at this hour - that ye might receive of him this word - which shall be a light unto the feet of the novice --

= **The Constant Companion** =

The Light which shall fall upon the feet of the novice - shall be from the lamp which He carries - - he goes before the novice that he might lead him safely into the Inner Temple - wherein he might find his own light --

= **In His Footsteps** =

I say unto thee: I am come that ye might be safe-guarded thru thy hours of trial and temptations - - lead thou - as I have led thee - and be ye as one on whose shoulders rests great responsibility --

= **Preparation** =

For this have I directed thee - for this have I sponsored thee - and it is now come when ye shall lead them - even as I have led thee -- So be it and Selah -- Therefore - I say unto thee: Be ye as one come alive - and ye shall walk knowingly - - ye shall know as I know - and ye shall not fail - neither shall ye want --

= The Light unto My Feet =

Mine lamp is trimmed and burning - it is the Light by which ye find thy way thru the shadows - the deep and dark shadows - which haunt the one which aspires to attain the height feign not wisdom - for wisdom is that which is to be the reward of the Victor - - the victory won - wisdom attained -- Let it be remembered that the wise one leads on - - the neophyte follows willingly --

This I would point out: There is none which bring thee against thy will - none to carry thee on their back -- Ye shall follow of thy own free will and strength -- Hear ye - and remember that which is said -- bear ye witness of me - and fear not - for I am with thee - and I shall not forsake thee -- Place thy hand firmly in mine - and I shall lead thee aright --

Forget not - that I am he which is Sent that ye be safeguarded thru the darkness - and my Light shall not fail thee -- Be ye responsive unto mine Voice - for I say: "Come - follow where I lead thee - and ye shall not fail"--

Recorded by Sister Thedra

= The Word of the Lord =

Sori Sori -- Let thine hand be mine hand - and ye shall give unto them which are prepared to receive - this mine word - for it shall profit them. This mine word is given unto them for their own sake - that they might know that which is given unto them <u>this day</u> -- So be it and Selah ---

= The Ages =

<u>This</u> <u>day</u> is a new day - and each has its place - its time - its part - - and all fits into the age - past - present and future --

The law is such that each day brings its own fulfillment - as does each age - - the age is but the many days - such as the weeks become years ---

= The Purpose =

Now I say - that ye are now come into <u>this</u> <u>age</u> for a <u>divine</u> purpose - that of fulfilling a law - the law under which ye come -- This law hast been given names varyingly - and names which are not always correct.

= Its not the End =

These are the days which have been foretold long ago - in ages past - - yet it is not the end of all the world - neither of the Earth - for I say unto thee: The Earth shall not perish! Neither shall She be finished in <u>this</u> <u>Age</u> - for She shall be delivered!

= Suffering =

This I would say - that there shall be trials and suffering - and there shall be wailing and cries for peace - - yet no peace shall be found within their plans - for they are not of a mind to accept peace --

= Futility =

Peace is not within them - they are of the mind to serve the dragon - - therefore I shall withdraw mine hand from them and they shall perish -

they shall learn well their lesson - - from their lessons shall they learn the way of peace - and the futility of war --

= A Lesson Learned =

So be it that they shall at last come to know the meaning of "Brotherhood"- the meaning of "Love ye one another"--

= Self Assurance =

Now for this day - I would speak unto thee - that ye might not suffer for them - or wait with them - - yet ye shall be mindful of their suffering.

= Atonement =

They shall be responsible for their own "sins" - - There shall be no place to hide - no cover for their nakedness - they shall stand naked before me - the Lord thy God -- They shall be weighed in the balance - and be found wanting

= Warning =

I say: The law hast been given - the law in its simplicity hast been made clear - that even the simple might understand.

= God's Grace =

Wherein is it said that - "Fools shall be raised up to do the Will of the Father which hast Sent me"- it is so - - and these shall be glorified above all the great and glorified of the Earth - which are as traitors unto their trust

= Messengers =

There are ones sent even as I - that they be warned of the dangers which lie ahead - - while they go headlong into battle - crying for blood -- I say unto them: "Lay down thy arms - and know ye that ye are brothers flesh of one flesh - brothers all - and ye hear me not!!"--

= I am Come =

This is the day of reckoning! I am Come! - That the Age be as none other -- I am Come that they might have Light - that they perish not --

= Voice in the Wilderness =

For this is given unto me - that they might be delivered of their own bondage -- While they turn from me and mine word - I am helpless to give unto them mine assistance -- I am come crying: "Awaken ye children of Earth! Awaken all ye nations of the Earth!"- Yet they heed not mine Voice - they turn a deaf ear unto me ---

= The Wicked =

Now I shall do that which I am to do - I shall withdraw mine hand - and they shall go the way of flesh - - and ye shall not <u>grieve</u> for them - for they shall be as ones prepared in the place wherein they shall go - for that which shall be given unto them to do --

= Slaughter =

They shall see the folly of their ways - they shall find therein the foolishness of sacrifice unto me - the futility of slaughter - hatred – envy.

= Sacrifice =

They shall know that the only profitable sacrifice is "Self" - and self-sacrifice is the only sacrifice acceptable unto the Father which hast Sent me --

= The Law =

They shall turn unto the Light crying for assistance - then they shall be heard and answered -- So be it as the law asks judgement - it is accorded as they are prepared to receive - - Justice rendered I say! for the Law is just!!

= Servants & Traitors =

This I would say unto thee: Serve ye the Light - which I Am - - Serve ye selflessly - and with all thy heart - giving unto me credit for being that which I am -- Know ye that I am come that <u>All</u> men be lifted up -- Yet I say: I am as one rejected by the traitors - and I find they are a rebellious lot - and they are as ones which have thrown over their own life belt --

= Deliverance =

They shall cry out - and they shall find no place of safety save in me -- They shall at last turn unto the Light and call - and <u>then</u> they shall find that the Light shall not fail them which seek - - They shall then be delivered from their bondage -- This is - "Repentance" -- Blest are they which turn unto the Light - - Blest are they which seek the Light - which I Am --

Recorded by Sister Thedra

= Greater Things Shall Ye Do =

Sori Sori -- This is mine time with thee - and ye shall be as one prepared to enter into the Inner Temple wherein I abide - - for this have I brot thee hence - - for this have I said: "Follow thou me"- for this have I led thee hither --

I bring thee into the place wherein ye are prepared to go -- I bring thee into the places wherein ye go - that ye be prepared for the Inner Temple wherein I abide –

= The Greater Capacity =

This I have said unto thee: "As ye prepare thyself - so shall ye receive"- Now I say: Thy time is come when ye shall be as one prepared for Greater things - and ye shall walk with me - counsel with me - and do that which I shall give unto thee to do --

Ye shall know well thy part - and ye shall not fail -- Ye shall bring them forth as ones prepared - - ye shall bring them in as the harvest - - ye shall find them which have gone astray - and ye shall prepare them even as thou hast been prepared --

Thy harvest shall be great - for the time is come when they shall come seeking the Light - - and ye shall find them ready to receive that which I have given unto thee for them -- So be it I shall bring them unto thee - and they shall heed that which ye say unto them --

They shall give heed unto thee - and they shall be as ones blest to heed -- Be ye as one blest - for ye shall not fail --

= Assurance =

Ye shall stand firm - and walk ye tall - - for I say unto thee: Mine hand is upon thee - and ye shall be as one in authority - for I have called thee forth and given unto thee the power and authority to speak in mine name - that which I give unto thee to say ---

= The Greater Sight =

Now it is come when ye shall see the plan set before thee -- <u>There is a plan</u> - which thou hast seen in part only - - yet thou shall see in Greater measure - and ye shall rejoice that ye have been given the Gift of Sight.

There is one which shall come unto thee - and he shall have within his hand the power and the authority to give unto thee that Gift of Sight --

= Responsibility =

Ye shall accept it in the name of the Father which hast Sent me -- Ye shall be as one on whose shoulders rests Great responsibility - for it brings with it (the Gift) Greater responsibility --

While I say: "it brings greater responsibility" - I have said: "As ye are prepared - so shall ye receive"--

Ye shall now go forth as one prepared for that responsibility ---

= Admonition =

Let not thy foot slip - for it is mine part to go before thee - that the way be prepared before thee - - and it is thy part to follow where I lead thee. So be it I say: "Come - follow ye me - the way I have prepared before thee"

Make strait the way of the Lord - and ye shall find that I have made the way before thee strait and accessible unto thee ---

= Temple of Charity =

It is now come when we have entered into the Temple of Charity - and therein ye shall find many which shall be unto thee great Light -- Ye shall be given instruction in the way of the Initiate - and ye shall know that which ye shall do - - and ye shall go forth renewed - as one prepared to enter into the next door which shall open before thee - - for it shall be as the open door before thee - and ye shall pass as one prepared --

I say: "Pass ye in"

So be it and Selah

Recorded by Sister Thedra

= The Time of Need =

Sori Sori --

Say unto them in mine name - that the time cometh swiftly - when they shall stand as ones shorn of all their vainglory - all their pride - all their selfishness --

They shall stand humbled before the Lord of Lords - - they shall be as little children - helpless - crying for bread - - for they shall be in need.

I say: "They shall be in need!"- for they have set into motion that which shall be unto them their undoing - so be it the law - - they shall reap what they have sown --

Be ye as mine mouth - mine Voice unto them - and give unto them this mine word -- I say: "They shall be in need!" - for they have turned their face from me - their Benefactor--

They have discredited me - and mine word - - they have been as the traitor unto themself - while I stand before them with hands outstretched --

They have rushed headlong into the pit -- They have been as ones prone to destruction -- They have fashioned for themself their own pit. They have given unto themself credit for being wise --

Let it suffice that I say unto them: "Turn from the way of war - seek ye the Light - which I Am - and be ye as ones prepared that I might enter in"--

Wherein is it said - that they have turned me out - shut the door in mine face - blasphemed the Name of the Father Which hast Sent me --

So be it that they shall come to know that which they do is the way of the dragon -- They shall turn from him and seek the Light - they shall stand as ones in need - - so be it I shall give unto them as they are prepared to receive

Let it profit them to turn from their way - and seek the Light - which shall be unto them Peace - - Peace shall be established within them - and they shall war no more --

For this do I stand by - ready to give assistance - and be unto them their assistant in the time of need -- Wait upon me in the time of thine youth - and I shall remember thee in thine old age --

Wherein is it said that - "They shall come unto me with clean hands"- - I say: "They shall lay down their arms - and be as ones prepared to accept me"- they shall be as ones prepared!

They shall be as ones on whose shoulders rests the responsibility of their own mis-used energy - their own "Sins"-- Let it be according unto the LAW --

While I say - they shall stand as ones humble before me - I say: They shall come as little children crying for bread - asking for sustenance of me -- then I shall give unto them as they are prepared to receive --

While I now say: They shall stand as ones shorn of their power - of their glory - vainglory - conceit - their boastings - - their aggression shall profit them nought - for they shall be brot low --

Bear ye in mind that there is no hiding place - no place can they hide from me - from the Father Which hast given them Life! They shall come to know that I Am He which is Sent that they might find Peace - Peace Eternal --

I say unto them: Turn from thy way - seek the Light - lay down thy arms - and give unto me credit for knowing that which I say unto thee.

Cast aside thy plans of aggression - and be ye as ones prepared for Peace -- I bring not Peace - - I bring unto thee a Plan - that Peace be established within thy heart --

Wait upon ME - serve ye the Light - and be ye as ones blest of Me for I am come that ye be blest -- For this do I say: "Come as one prepared to receive Me". For this do I reveal mineself at <u>this time</u> -- Behold ye the Glory of the "Lord"- for He hast spoken that ye be blest Behold ye the Way of Peace - - Behold ye the way of destruction!

For it lies before thee! I say: "Turn ye and be ye as ones alert unto Mine Word -- Heed that which I say -- PERISH NOT! WANT NOT!"

Recorded by Sister Thedra

= His Will Made Manifest =

Sori Sori --

Be ye as one blest to receive of me - this my Word - - record it for them - that they might be prepared to receive me in the name of Mine Father which hast sent me --

As His Will I come - for I am His Will made manifest -- It is now come when ye shall go forth - and ye shall do that which I give unto thee to do - and ye shall not falter - or fail --

Ye shall walk fearlessly - and with surety -- ye shall do that which I give unto thee to do - and ye shall be as mine hand and foot made manifest --

For this have I prepared thee -- Ye shall bring them into the place which I have prepared for them - - and as they have prepared themself so shall they receive --

It is said: They shall choose where they go - yet it is said: They prepare themself for the place they shall go - they shall be put into the place they belong -- Each shall be in his proper environment - for he shall be in like company --

I say unto them: "Seek ye the Light" - and they shall find--

They shall first make ready themself -- They shall put from themself all pettiness/ childishness/ foolishness/ and they shall be as ones which are prepared to receive me - *then* I shall touch them - and give unto them in capacity as they are able to receive --

It is said: Come as an empty vessel - - they come - bringing their own cups - filled with the offal of their own - - their cups are filled - that no more can they contain - they are as the sealed vessel -- I cannot put 'new wine in the old cup' for it is not of the same vintage --

The opinions of man hast been unto him his own - not mine -- I say I am not of his making - of his "Vintage" - of his imaging - - he hast had many visions of me -- Many concepts hast he had - yet he hast not known me as I Am - for I am not limited as *man* - - I Am free - "FREE" I say!

Man would limit me - like unto himself - for he walks as one limited for he knows not that he is free - he hast not as yet awakened - he is as one sleeping - - yet he shall come forth as one awake - he shall walk free - as one unbound - - for this do I say - Awaken!

I come that he awaken -- So be it he shall hear me - and bestir himself - and he shall grow in strength and stature - he shall become of age - and then he shall receive of me his part - which hast been held in trust for him - until he hast reached maturity --

Man - as such is mature - - the un-mature is as the child - therefore I say: "Mine children Awaken!" and be ye blest that ye be among the Awakened -- So be it and Selah --

Let them come - let them be as the ones which have the will to learn hear - see - and receive -- Let them put their hand to the plow - - let them earn their passport - let them prove themself - then I shall do mine part --

They shall come as a little child - as one asking for bread -- They shall be as one humbled - shorn of all <u>self-glory</u> - they shall know themself to be in need -

They shall be in <u>want</u> - - They shall be as ones serviceable in Mine House - for I say: I set up Mine House in Mine Father's name - and it is in His Name that I come - - and I say: No laggards shall dwell in the House of the Lord --

Neither shall a liar - a thief - a deceiver - a tattler nor a hypocrite dwell therein --

I say: They shall be as one prepared to dwell in the House of the Lord --

They shall be as ones responsible for the part given unto them -- They shall be as ones which are prepared for a part - and it shall be given - and accepted - with gratitude and joy - - it shall be done according to the best of their ability - and they shall be obedient unto the law - which is just --

They shall waver not concerning their preparation - they shall at all times be as ones responsible for their own actions - and deeds - words and the results thereof --

They shall walk upright - knowing they are as ones responsible - knowing that I am the Master - that I am Sent that they have Light - - that I have declared unto them the LAW - - that I have set up mine Shield and Banner - under which they shall serve with honor and dignity -- I say: They shall honor mine Servants - mine Priests - mine Priestesses - Prophets - and Ambassadors - - for these I have sent unto thee that ye be lifted up -- Ye shall honor them - and be likewise honored for thy trust-worthiness -- So be it that ye shall be as one remembered - and numbered - and ye shall be as one acceptable and useful in Mine House --

So be it I say: Prepare thyself - that ye might enter into the Inner Temple wherein I abide -- So be it and Selah --

Now I say unto thee: Ye shall enter into the place wherein ye shall go - - as the outer temple - as the entrance of mine Temple is hidden from the outer temple - first ye pass the outer before ye might see the Inner --

The inner is forbidden unto thee - before ye have passed within the portals of the outer - - therefore I say: Prepare thyself for to enter into mine place of abode --

Ye shall learn obedience and Love - then ye shall be as one prepared to serve Me with all thy strength - all thy heart and mind -- Now ye shall place thine hand in mine - and I shall lead thee safely and with surety --

Be ye as one blest to learn well thy lessons - - and praise ye the Name of Solen Aum Solen - for He is the cause of thy being --

Let thy hand be mine - thy foot be mine - thy VOICE MINE - and ye shall be blest of Him which is The Father Eternal --

Holy - Holy - is His Name - and none other shall be glorified - none other above Him - neither below - - None other - I SAY!

Falter not - - put not thy foot into a hole - for there are many pitfalls many temptations -- Be ye alert - watchful - and remember - I am with thee - -

I am He which is Sent - -

So be it I am the Gatekeeper - -

I am the Porter at the Gate --

Recorded by Sister Thedra

= Tests =

Sori Sori --

Bear in mind that which I have said - and remember well that which I have given unto thee - for it is thy Shield and thy Buckler --

THE WORD is given unto thee that ye might be sustained in the hour of thy struggle - in the hour of thy trials and tests --

Tested ye shall be - - trials ye shall have - and ye shall be as ones blest to remember well that which hast been given unto thee ---

Fear not - for I have said unto thee: I am with thee - - ye have but to remember that which I have said - and hold high thy head - - walk ye with surety of purpose --

Praise ye the Name of Solen Aum Solen - - Know ye that nought of harm can come nigh unto thee - for I am come that ye be lifted up -- So be it and Selah ---

Return unto me that which I have given unto thee - and I shall give unto thee in greater measure - for greater Gifts have I for thee - GREATER Gifts I say - have I kept for thee - - and ye shall find that which I have kept for thee shall surpass <u>anything</u> thou hast ever imaged.

Thy Gifts shall be as the Stars in thy Crown - each shall be different from the others - and ye shall be as one prepared to receive these Gifts for none other shall receive them ---

Now ye shall be as one which has the power and the authority to go into the Inner Temple - the Holy of Holies - to go where I go - - and nothing shall be hidden from thee - for ye shall be as a "Son of the Living God"- and He - the Father - shall place upon thy brow the Crown of the Victor -- So be it and Selah --

Fortune thyself the Crown of Victory - return ye unto thy place of going out - receive thy Crown of the Father - and be ye as one which hast returned Victoriously -- Let it be as the Father hast willed it ---

= The Lost =

This I would say unto thee: There is not one amongst thee that hast been forgotten - - yet there are as ones which have wandered in the wilderness as ones lost - they have lost their way - they cry: "Which way - which way - which way" - for they fear - and pay no heed unto the Voice which cries: "COME - Come unto Me and be ye as one blest. Come unto Me and find peace"---

= The Way of the Dragon =

They turn unto the ways of the dragon - they ask of the sooth-sayers - they seek the necromancers - the astrologers - the numerologers - the magician and the many which trade in men's souls - - the ones who traffic in black magic --

Pity! Pity I say - - and they know not that they are trapt - they know not that which they do -- So be it I say: They shall first turn from them and seek the Light - for the Light which I Am shall be unto them their salvation -- Therefore - it behooves me to say unto them which seek the Light: "Be ye as one aware - be ye alert - put thy foot not in a hole - lest thou be entrapt"--

Seek ye first the Light and ye shall find - - seek ye the way unto the Father's House -- Be ye blest to find - - for this have I come - that ye might find thy way - that ye might return with me -- So be it as the Father hast willed it -- Amen and Selah --

Recorded by Sister Thedra

= The Harvest =

Sori Sori --

Bear in mind that the time is now come when man shall now be as fortuned that which they have prepared for themself - they shall now be as ones which gather their harvest - - for it is said: "As ye have sown so shall ye reap"- - there is the season of sowing past - now is the season of reaping --

This season is upon them -- It is said that they have prepared their own cup for themself - yet they proffer it unto their brother - - and they cry for peace? Wherein have they given the cup of peace? Wherein have they been at peace within themself?

= Bitter Cup =

Let it be as they have prepared themself - - they have prepared for themself the cup of bitters - - let them partake - and they shall drink the last bitter dreg -- And when they have drunken thereof - they shall find it bitter - THEN - they shall prepare the cup of oil - which shall serve as the healing balm for their wounds -- Then they shall turn unto the Light for their help - and they shall be given in accord to their capacity.

= Results =

Call it the law - call it what ye will - for it is the law - - as ye are prepared so shall ye receive -- Let not thy hand slip - neither thy tongue nor thy foot --

While I say ye shall not let thy hand slip - neither thy tongue - it is given unto me to see them giving a hand unto the enemy - - they give comfort unto the enemy - - they go forth to do a <u>good</u> <u>deed</u> - and put their foot in a hole - and find themself entrapt - - I say "entrapt" for they have prepared for themself the trap - they have spoken words which were not of me - and they have falsified that which I <u>have</u> said - they have misused mine words to their own end --

= False Teachers =

They have put words into mine mouth - which I spit out - for I say unto them: I do not give unto thee power to put words into mine mouth - neither do I give unto them power to speak for me - for they are betrayers - - they are not of me - they are not the fruit of mine labors - nor are they of mine flock --

They are of the damned - they are of the evil one - which hast betrayed himself - they follow him - THEY plan the wars --

= Self Glory =

They give of themself that they be satisfied - they gratify themself with blood - hatred and death - - I say - death! Yea - they are the father of destruction - they plan destruction - they are as ones which have planned the destruction of All which serve the Light --

= Alertness =

Be ye - O Mine Children - ever watchful - ever alert! on guard that ye put not thy foot into their trap -- Remember that I am thy Shield and thy Buckler -- I am He which is Sent to deliver thee out -- Give the enemy no footing - no power over thee and I shall do mine part - - I shall sustain thee in the hour of trials and temptations -- So be it and Selah ---

= Worthiness =

Be ye as one trust worth - betray not thyself - for it is given unto me to see them falter - and fall by the way -- They weary of mine sayings - and they fear for themself - - they faint by the way - and no heed do they give unto the WORD which I give unto them - - they think themself wise --

Yet I say: THEY HAVE BETRAYED THEMSELF

They have closed Me out

Now I say they shall wait --

= The Reward =

Blest is he which comes this day -- Blest is he which goes where I go - and he shall find favor with me -- He shall be blest as none other -- So be it and Selah --

Recorded by Sister Thedra

= Watch! =

Sori Sori --

Be ye as the hand of me - and record that which I say unto thee - - for they shall bear witness of mine words - and it shall profit them --

Say unto them in mine name - that they shall see their towers topple their ships shall rust in their berths - their guns shall sit as reminders of their foolishness - and they shall find that their machines of the air shall be as the poor part of travel - for they shall fail them - - they shall be as ones helpless - and know not which way to turn - - they shall find with all their getting - they have not gotten wisdom --

Now there shall be a great cry go up - and it shall reverberate thruout the land - and it shall be as nothing heard before - it shall be as the cry in the night --

Their places shall be as ones poured over by the enemy - - they shall be over-run - and it shall be as nothing seen before - it shall be the sign of the times --

For the enemy shall over-run the land - and he shall be as the enemy therefore it is said: Prepare thyself - PREPARE thyself!! - For the time is come when ye shall see that the enemy is not to be satisfied - he is the ENEMY - and not to be reconciled! He hast the will to destroy - lay waste - and put asunder the Rites and the Truth of man - as given of the Mighty Council --

He hast gone so far as to bring bloodshed of the little ones - to make lawful the slaughter of the unborn - - the war in which men are slain is honorable by comparison -- I say: It is the dragon abroad in the land -- See ye that which he does - and bear in mind that he is the evil one - the evil which is the oppressor - which holds man bound - and which is the enemy!

Dare ye stand up and be counted - for I say unto thee: Hold ye steadfast and know that I am not to be turned aside - I am with thee to the end - for ye shall stand with me in this - and I shall shield thee --

I say: TURN NOT FROM ME - FOR I AM THY SHIELD AND THY BUCKLER --

I Am that I Am -

Recorded by Sister Thedra

= Implementation =

Sori Sori --

Be ye as the hand made manifest for this part which I shall give unto them which are prepared to receive it --

Let them know that which I say unto them by this means -- I say - it is for their own good that I speak out this day - - yet they are not about the Father's business as I am - and they heed not the Voice which cries out unto them

= Where Lord? =

While it is said that they <u>shall</u> heed - and they shall be brot up short - - they have turned from me - seeking signs and wonders of men - asking of them peace! - - and they know not that peace is not to be found at their council tables --

They cry: "Peace - Peace - Peace"- yet they are not at peace - - peace is not in them - they have not followed in the way of PEACE --

= The Boomerang =

It is now come when the greatest of all suffering shall come upon the nations and the peoples - for they have set into motion the energy - and that which they have set into motion shall rebound upon them - - they shall be as ones on whose shoulders rests the responsibility of their own actions -- Many shall suffer the consequences of their own "Sins" - their own ways -- And there shall be children yet unborn - which shall suffer from their deeds - so wontonly committed -- They shall be as the innocent - yet their day shall bring forth fruit which shall be sweet in their stomach - they shall eat thereof and find it sweet ---

= 666 vs O =

From this time forward it shall be given unto thee to see them yield unto the cry for blood - and they shall yield unto the cry as never before Ones shall rush headlong into the streets in frenzied passion - seeking blood -- They shall run as mad men - and they shall not be satisfied - for there shall be no satisfaction to be found in their hatred -- In their way - in their "hours" of terror they shall destroy themself - - the way in which they go shall be the way of darkness and destruction -- They shall be as ones responsible for that which they do - for I have warned them - - for ages past I have sent mine Emissaries - mine prophets - mine Messengers amongst them as mine Voice - mine feet made manifest upon the Earth - - And they have heeded not the Voice - the Word - - They have slain the prophets - the messengers - - and Emissaries have been slain - persecuted - ridiculed - and turned out - - they have been as outcasts --

= The Traitors =

They have given unto them the cup of gall - and found that they themselves have to drink of the cup which they have given unto the prophets and messengers and emissaries --

Poor are they - - with all their knowledge they have not been "Wise" they have boasted - and strutted before men - and they have given unto me no credit for being the "Head of State"- the Counselor - for they have not taken my Counsel --

They have not heeded my Counsel - neither have they accepted ME as their "Head of State" -- I have said: "I am the Founder of this land of Liberty" - and I have brot forth a <u>Great</u> <u>Nation</u> --

= The House Divided =

It is said: "In God We Trust" - yet wherein have they given unto Me the credit - the Power the Glory?

Wherein do they sing the songs of Praise unto the Lord? and wherein do they say: "Give us Liberty or give us death?

Now they shall find that they have portioned out the bitter cup for themself - the which they shall drink - and they shall find it bitter indeed. Indeed I say: IT SHALL BE BITTER!! So be it the law is exacting - "The way of sin is death"--

I am come as One Sent - crying: "Come ye out from among them - Come ye - follow me - and be ye not part of them"- yet they follow after the one which would lead them down to destruction --

While I say: "they follow the dark one - which would lead them down unto destruction" - I say they have the choice which way they go.

= Which Way? =

They which follow him willingly shall perish - - they which turn from him shall find peace -- Yet I say - the way of peace is not to be found in flesh - for flesh is not the way of peace --

Peace I give unto them which follow me - - and I say I shall return unto mine place of abode in peace - and nought of darkness shall there be wherein I go -- I am He which is come that they be delivered from bondage - and that they might know PEACE --

They shall choose this day which way they go -- So be it I have spoken and I have been heard by some - - some have given unto me credit for being that which I Am - - others have set foot against me and closed the door that I might not enter in -- Unto these I say: "The way of the rebellious is hard indeed - the way of the wonton is destruction".

= Peace =

Blest are the ones which walk with me - and serve the Light - which are mine servants - - I say: "Blest are Mine Servants for they shall be blest of Mine Father which hast Sent Me -- So be it and Selah -- Praise ye the Name of Solen Aum Solen - Unto Him ALL THE PRAISE AND THE GLORY!!

So let it be forever and forever -

Recorded by Sister Thedra

= Memory =

Be ye as one on whose head I place mine hand - and be ye blest of me and by me -- Let thy hand be mine hand - and ye shall record that which I say unto thee - and it shall serve the purpose for which it is recorded.

So be it that the time is come when ye shall do the work which I do. Ye shall go where I send thee - ye shall say that which I give unto thee to say - and ye shall know that which ye do to be that which is Mine work --

Pay ye heed unto that which I say - and be ye obedient unto that which I give unto thee - for it shall be according to the law --The law is just - and according to thy preparation so shall ye receive -- So be it and Selah ---

= Fear Not =

Fret not over thy part - for it shall be given unto thee to know that which ye are to do - that which ye have done - - and thy memory shall be restored unto thee - and ye shall remember that which is done in the hours of thy sleep - for ye shall have the memory of thy time with me - Is it not said - that - thy memory shall be restored - it is so -- So let it be as the Father wills it - - for this do I say: "Follow Me - fear not for I shall lead thee safely"--

= The Initiate =

Now I say unto thee: Bring thyself - and I shall accept thee as the sacrificial offering - - I shall give unto thee as I have received -- Ye shall be blest as I have been blest - - ye shall walk with surety - knowingly ---

Ye shall ponder mine words - and ye shall not fail -- Place thy hand in mine and I shall take thee thru the shadows safely - and then ye shall do as I have done - - ye shall assist others which follow after thee - - for this have I given unto thee assistance -- So be it - as ye receive so shall ye give - let it be - - for this do I give unto thee mine Mantle --

The Mantle of Gold I shall place upon thy shoulders - and ye shall wear it becomingly and knowingly -- Ye shall be as one on whose head rests the Crown of the Sun - and ye shall be as one prepared for the Greater part - - ye shall do greater things than thou hast dreamed of -- Ye shall stand tall - walk with surety - and go where I lead thee -- Ye shall heal the sick in mine name - and ye shall give unto the Father all the Praise and the Glory -- So be it and Selah --

= Clean the Cup =

Put aside all thy puny ideas - concepts of me - and the part which hast been given unto thee - and know ye that Greater work shall ye do - Greater things than these shall ye do - for it is needful that ye be brot out of darkness—No more shall ye walk blindly - no more shall ye wander in darkness - no more shall ye weary - no more shall ye want - So be it I have spoken and I am speaking - and I am not finished - - I shall speak again and again -- So be it and Selah --

Recorded by Sister Thedra

= The Messenger =

Sori Sori -- Be ye as mine hand made manifest unto them which have the will to follow me - the way I go --

Be ye as one blest to receive this mine word for them - - let it be recorded as I give it unto thee - and it shall be unto them much Light.

= The Message =

When they have accepted that which I have given unto them - and when they have done that which I have given unto them to do - they shall find that I am prepared to give unto them in greater measure --

= The Work Goes On =

They shall be as ones prepared to receive in greater capacity - for it shall be increased in great proportions -- None shall gainsay mine word for there is a Host which shall bear witness of mine Word - and that which I now do - - that which I have done - - and I say: I am but begun for I shall show mine hand unto them which follow where I lead them. So be it and Selah ---

= ? ? ? =

Wherein have I failed thee? Wherein hast it been given unto me to be found wanting? Wherein hast it been given unto me to be found sleeping?

= Reality =

When they awaken unto me - they shall know that I am present - that I am here - that I am not afar off in a corner -- I am not limited to any place - be it in the world of man - planet or galaxy - - I am free --

= Freedom =

It is said: Prepare thyself to go where I go - prepare thyself to do that which I do - and ye shall be free as I am free --

Freedom! Freedom! is that which is earned - "EARNED!" I say -- Thy Victory is thy Freedom --

= The Way =

Hast it not been said: This is thy concern? Hast it not been said - service is thy part? Serve Me - and thy life shall be secure - for I AM the Life the Light - - <u>this</u> is the WAY ---

= The Oneness =

Wherein is it said: "Be ye as mine hand and foot made manifest"- - it behooves me to say: "As ye serve ME so do ye serve the Father which hast given unto thee being --

= Awareness =

Be ye mindful of Him - and ye shall bless thyself in the remembrance of Him - - Praise ye the Name of Solen Aum Solen ---

= The Detours =

While ye <u>shall</u> be as one prepared to follow me - I say: ye have been as ones long on thy return - and ye have been as wanderers in the valley of despair - and ye have been as ones walking in darkness - - ye have dragged thy legirons with thee - and now ye shall lay aside thy legirons/ thy possessions - yea - even thy opinions which hast been unto thee as an <u>unopened</u> book - - they have not been the 'open book'- for they have been opinions - not <u>revelations</u> --

= The Empty Cup =

While I say: Put aside all thy preconceived opinions of me and about me - I say - Come - prove me for what I Am -- See me - Know me - walk with me - and I shall give thee comprehension -- I shall open up thine eyes - and ye <u>shall</u> see! and Know --

= Try Me! =

For this do I say: "Come"- for this do I say: "Walk ye with me - test me try me - and ye shall come of thy own free will"-- So let it be --

Recorded by Sister Thedra

= The Pronouncement =

Sori Sori -- Mine hand I place upon thy head and I pronounce the Word and ye receive the word in the name of the Father - the Son - and the Spirit --

The Spirit in which it is given is the Spirit in which ye receive the Word -- The Holy Spirit in which I come unto thee is the Spirit in which ye have thy being -- The Holy Spirit is that which animates the physical body with which ye now record the Word which I give unto thee --

= Discipline =

It is for thy sake that I say unto thee: Awaken and record that which I say -- "Bear ye witness of that which I say" - it is for thy own sake that I call thee at this hour when ye obey mine touch--

Ye have been alert unto the touch and responded promptly -- Now I say unto thee: Ye shall have greater responsibility - for I shall require of thee Greater Service - Greater responsibility and alertness -- So be it as ye are prepared to receive -- Ye shall now be as one prepared for the next part - and it shall be as none other - for ye shall go into fields afar and ye shall soar as the eagle - and ye shall bring back the memory of thy sojourn - - and ye shall be as one prepared to do that which I give unto thee to do -- I shall lead thee safely and surely - - fear not - for I am with thee -- So be it and Selah --

Recorded by Sister Thedra

= Acceptance =

Sori Sori -- Let that which I say be recorded for them which have the mind or will to follow where I go -- This is mine word unto them - and they shall neither add unto - or take away - they shall be as ones mindful of mine <u>Counsel</u> - for I have given unto them such counsel that shall profit them --

Wherein is it said that they shall obey the law -- The <u>Word</u> is given unto them that they be lifted up -- So be it they shall accept it in the Name of the Father - and the Son which I Am --

They shall be as ones blest of the Father - and the Light which I Am. They shall be as ones which have received the Word unto themselves, they shall take it unto themself - and be as ones blest --

<u>Then</u> - I shall touch <u>them</u> and they shall know that they have been touched -- They shall commune with me - and then they shall give unto me ear - and they shall be as ones prepared to accept me as I Am --

There are ones which claim to know me - yet they have not heard mine Voice - neither have they accepted the Word -- There are ones which are the hands and feet of me made manifest - which do mine work - mine part - which is the part that I have given unto them - - these are mine "Servants"- for they serve me - even as I serve <u>Mine</u> Father which hast Sent Me --

So be it that I am mindful of these Mine Servants - for it is needful that I am mindful of them -- I give unto them that which is needful - that which serves well the Great and <u>Divine</u> Plan --

THEY ARE AS MINE HAND & FOOT - therefore I have need of them - - it is necessary that I be watchful and mindful of them - - I say: They are never alone --

While they go and come within the "Shadows" as ones unknowing they walk with <u>surety</u> - they fear not - neither do they ask the rewards of men - they follow willingly and joyfully -- They ask not self-reward, Glory - nor do they fear any man's scorn -- They are as ones prepared to go where I lead them - for they know that I Am with them --

They seek the Light - they are as ones led into the Light - - they are the ones blest of the Light which I Am. They bring unto me themselves.

They ask of no man aught -- They weary not of their trials - their part -They do that which I give unto them with a glad heart - and with joy - they give unto the Father Solen Aum Solen all the Praise and the Glory.

Wherein is it said that none come unprepared - - for these are as the ones which have <u>not</u> prepared to enter into mine place of abode --

Hast it not been said: "As ye prepare thyself - SO SHALL YE RECEIVE" -- Yet they <u>think</u> I speak foolish repetitions! It is not so - for I am not given unto foolishness or idle sayings --

I am the Counselor of Counselors - - I am come that they might be <u>sobered</u>! - - that they might know that I Am about MINE FATHER'S BUSINESS! So be it and Selah --

When they are sobered - and are of the metal which I can accept into mine place of abode - then I shall do mine part -- Yet I say: I am not deceived by their flowery speech - their ceremony - creeds - customs - by the color of their skin - their honeyed words of praise - - neither am I blind unto their vain repetitions -- I am aware of that which they do - that which they say - that which they ARE! they deceive me not -- So be it I am the Light of the WORLD -- Be ye as one on whose head I place mine hand and I shall bless thee with Mine Being -- So be it and Selah --

Recorded by Sister Thedra

= God's Word =

Sori Sori --

Be ye as the hand of me made manifest unto them - and record this mine Word - that they might know that which I say unto thee --

Ye shall go into the place wherein there are ones prepared to receive thee - and ye shall give unto them as I have given unto thee -- Ye shall be as the lamp unto their feet -- and ye shall go unto them even as I have come unto thee - - for this have I prepared thee -- So be it and Selah --

Now ye shall be as one qualified - one prepared - and ye shall not fail - for I shall be with thee every step of the way - - I shall sustain thee and ye shall be glad for thy preparation -- So be it and Selah - - this is my word unto thee --

Now I shall speak unto them which ask for Light: Ye shall be blest to receive of this one which I have prepared - for she hast been as one true unto herself - as one tried - tested - and proven trust worth --

Now she shall go forth as one prepared to assist thee - - for this have I placed mine Seal upon her - and I have given unto her the "WORD" - and she shall use it for the Good of All mankind -- So be it and Selah - This shall be unto thee mine Word - and it shall not be made void - for no man shall say me NAY -- I have spoken and so shall it be - for I am He which is come that there be Light -- So let it be -- I Am that I Am

Recorded by Sister Thedra

= Bonea =

Bonea speaking unto thee: It is for the good of all that I speak at this time - for I come that I add my blessing unto theirs - that all be blest --

This is the word which I bring: The time is now come when I shall speak out - and the word shall go forth that they might have it - for the work which shall be accomplished in a short while -- Contact shall be made - and many adjustments shall be made - then the real work shall begin -- The work shall be that of awakening the sleepers --

They shall be brot to know that they are in need of knowledge - that they are in bondage - and need assistance - - then as they ask and seek the assistance which we are prepared to offer - then we shall come forth as ones prepared to assist in love - compassion and wisdom --

Yet they first must ask - and seek help - - and by so doing they bless themself --

It is with great joy that we are able to reach out our hand in assistance --

The time swiftly approaches when they shall lament their slothfulness and slowness -- While many shall think themself wise - and they shall be found wanting - I say: many shall lament their slothfulness - and seek the assistance of the Host which stands ever ready to assist --

The people of Earth stand on the brink of self-destruction as never before - and we know their need - - while they know not that they are not alone - - they know not that which is being done in the realms of

Light - that they might be spared - that the ones which <u>Seek</u> the Light be brot out --

They shall be brot out and put into their proper place - each in his proper place wherein he has prepared himself for -- There is no injustice in this - for it is by their own choice - and preparation - that he prepares himself for his place --

When he finds himself in his place - the knowledge that he has prepared himself for such a place - shall be given unto him - and he shall learn well that it is the law - "As ye are prepared so shall ye receive"--

When he has been prepared for greater things - they shall not be withheld from him - he shall receive unto his preparation --

Now it shall come to pass that one shall walk among them which seek the Light - and he shall find them and mark them - he shall touch them and quicken then - and they shall come alive - and then they shall know that they have not been alert unto the activity which goes on round about them - - that they have been blind unto that which is being done - accomplished while they slept -- So be it and Selah ---

Let it be the time of awakening - - for this are <u>we</u> sent forth - - so shall it be a glad day --

Let it bear fruit --

I am come that it might be — as the Father hast willed it --

Recorded by Sister Thedra

= He shall Turn the Key =

Sori Sori -- For this day let it be said that none shall enter into the Holy of Holies unprepared - for it is given unto me to know -- I am come that the way be made clear before them which seek the Light -- There are many which come into this place - which are as ones prepared to assist the ones which are now within flesh --

Flesh - is the part wherein they are given to want - and wherein they are given assistance from us - here in our place of abode --

While they know not from whence cometh their assistance - I say: We from this realm of Light give assistance unknown unto them - - for they see not the hand which directs the affairs of them which seek the Light -- They are guided - directed and sustained by the Hand of God -

While they which turn away find their way hard indeed - they too shall come to know that the Hand of God moves in ways they know not.

They shall come to know - for it is said: Every knee shall bow - and every voice shall praise Him - for it is So - - Let it Be ---

While it is given unto man of Earth to be a wayward lot - it is given unto us to be watchful of his progress and of his goings and comings - he hast wandered in darkness --

Now it is come when he wearies of his darkness - and he cries out for assistance - - it shall be given unto him and he shall be glad - for he hast within his hand the Key which shall unlock his prison doors - which shall fly open at his own touch -- He shall turn the Key and the door shall stand open before him - and he shall know that which he hast not known - - he shall be blest to know - for it is said: as he is prepared so shall he receive -- So be it and Selah --

I am come that he be blest of me and by me - for I am One of the Host which stands ready to assist ---

No man hast seen the end of the / Light - the Power - the Wisdom - the Plan - for it is not done / finished - - IT IS NOT FINISHED!

For there is Work to be done - - WORK! I say --

When the body of flesh is put aside - I say: there is yet work to be done - for work is the Key to rest - peace and progress -- Joy comes thru work - - recreation is but part of work and construction --

Construction is but the result of work and play -- When the play and work are combined in wisdom and balance - it can be constructive.

While there are ones which know not the meaning of work <u>or</u> play they know not the wisdom - neither the joy of / --

For it is with joy that we serve the Light - that we do things in order and with wisdom - and in harmony - for there is no dis-harmony in our place of abode -- So be there Peace!

= **Peace** =

Wherein is it said: Peace shall abide within them which enter herein - - So be it that none enter unprepared -- Wherein is it said: Prepare thyself for to enter into the place wherein there is Peace profound --

Place thine hand in mine and I shall show thee that which ye have not seen - for this am I sent - - for it shall be shown unto thee - for no pen can print the beauty which thine eye can behold - - no tongue can speak the word which thy eye can behold - - no joy can be conveyed unto thee - as thou alone can feel and experience -- Therefore I say: Come and Know -- So let it suffice that I am come that ye might Know as I Know -- So be it and Selah --

Such is mine word unto thee at this hour - - while it is yet not day - I say: ye shall arise refreshened – and ye shall be glad -- So be it and Selah –

Recorded by Sister Thedra

PEACE

= The Door =

Sori Sori --

Be ye as prepared for a new part which <u>is</u> prepared for thee - and it shall follow the part which is now being made ready --

Let it suffice that it is now prepared - and ye shall give it unto them as ye receive it -- So be it and Selah --

= Do Not Edit =

Care shall be taken - inasmuch as it shall be new unto thee - and it shall be as none other -- Yet - it shall be given as it is given unto thee - without any change -- Ye shall <u>not</u> edit it - neither change the letters - neither the words -- So be it that I am the Author and the Finisher of Mine Works -- So be it and Selah --

Ye shall add that which ye will - yet it is enuf to say - that it is the Father's Will that this work go forward in His Name -- So be it that all shall be blest to read - see - and comprehend - the fullness of that which is being done - and accomplished herein -- So be it and Selah -

Now ye shall be as one on whose shoulders rests Greater responsibility - for I shall give unto thee a part for them - and it shall be as none other --

Now - ye shall have the first part -- so be it separate from all others. This part shall be called:

- Peace -

And it shall have upon the Door - the Crown and the Cross - the Cross beneath the Crown - - The Door shall be as one closed --

The Crown shall rest above the center - - the Cross shall be in the center –

- Closed is the Door -

Crown above the Cross - like unto the Emerald Cross - - the Crown <u>just above</u> -- Just above these shall be the word "PEACE" - no other shall appear --

While it shall appear a small portion - I say: It is important -- So be it - and Selah -- I shall give it unto thee - assistance -- Fear not - for I am thy Director - and I shall direct thee –

- Peace -

= The Calling =

Sori Sori -- This is the beginning of a new part - which shall be given unto them -- And for this do I say unto thee: Give it unto them as ye receive it - and as they are prepared to receive it -- Give it not before they have received the foregoing parts - for therein is a Plan - the wisdom which is yet unknown - or revealed unto them -- It shall in time be revealed - for we are not without foresight -- We find them which are prepared - and we give unto them as they are prepared to receive - for there is a work to be done - and there is a time in which to do it --

There is a Plan - and the Plan shall be brot to its fullness - and they shall <u>then</u> - see that which they have done - and wherein they have labored - to bring forth the finish of the Plan - - for it shall be as all parts fit together - into One Whole - and no part shall be out of place or missing --

They shall bring their parts - and place them together with the parts of Mine other Servants - and then they shall know that they have been as ones responsible for the parts given unto them <u>by</u> <u>Me</u> -- And too - they shall be glad they have served Me of their own account And it behooves them this day - to hear that which I say - for the time swiftly approaches when they shall be called for an accounting - and they shall stand as ones accountable for that which they have done with Mine Word - - how they have used it - - and it shall be unto their credit when they have heard - and obeyed the Word - and when they have been unto their calling true --

= The Word Ineffable =

For have I not called them - - have I not given unto them the Word Infallible - Immaculate?

Have they heard - obeyed - and acted within it? Have they turned unto Me - and given heed unto that which I have said?

Have they read with their eyes blinded - and laid aside the pages - and waited for Mine Approach?

Is it not said - that I send one before Me to herald Mine Coming? - And they shall first accept the Word? - And Mine Messenger - Mine Emissary - then - I shall approach them - when they are prepared to receive ME?

= Who Shall Receive? =

This is Mine Word - and they which have heeded - seen - and heard that which I have said - and the ones which have given unto Me themself - their heart - their hand - and served Me willing - and without thot of self - shall be as ones blest to receive Me - and of Me -- So be it and Selah --

Such is Mine Word unto them -- This shall be the first of this New Part - and it shall be separate from that which hast gone before -- Now I say - it behooves them to give unto Me credit for Knowing that which I am about - and no man shall deny Me Mine parts - for I Am of Mine Father Sent that they be brot out of bondage -- So be it I am about Mine Father's Business -- So be it - Amen - and Selah --

= The Firm Foundation =

Sori Sori -- Upon this Foundation I have set Mine Temple - - upon this Temple I have placed Mine Seal - - and I have placed before thee the "Book of Life" - and therein is thy name written - - for it is so decreed by the Father - that ye shall stand with Me upon Mine High Holy Mount and be blest as I am blest -- So be it and Selah --

Cease not thy vigilance - bless thyself by thy vigilance -- Stay not the tide - for it bringeth good tidings -- Be ye as one blest to go forth upon the tide - for it beareth thee Great performings - and the Light shall be unto thee all things -- So be it - and Selah --

Rest in the knowing that I am with thee - that I am thy Shield and thy Buckler --

Accept that which I have prepared for thee - for I set before thee a table bearing rich viands - and thy cup is filled - and it shall overflow - They which cometh shall drink of the overflow - and be filled - so abundantly shall ye be blest!

They shall come seeking - asking - and respond to thy speaking - for thy words shall be Mine - and ye shall Know that which ye say - - for have I not ordained thee - and brot thee forth as Mine Hand Maiden?

I say - I have set Mine Temple on a firm Foundation - and I have placed Mine Seal upon Mine Temple - and I am satisfied - for Mine time is come -- And I shall lift up Mine Banner - and it shall not be trodden under foot - for no man shall gainsay Mine Word -- So shall I do a Wondrous Work - and they shall behold in Me the Light which I AM -- And they shall come to Know that which I say - and they shall marvel at their slowness -- So be it that I Am He - which is Sent - that there be Light -- So be it and Selah --

= Authorization =

Sori Sori -- Mine hand I place upon thee in Holy Benediction - and I speak the Word - and ye shall hear that which I say - and ye shall give it unto them - as they are prepared to receive it --

For I have prepared thee as Mine Priestess - that ye might give unto them in full measure - - and they shall receive it in Mine Name - for I have given unto thee the power and the Authority to speak for Me --

Now they shall be as the ones to receive thee - the Word - then - they shall be blest to receive Me -- And when they have prepared themself - I shall step forward - and bless them as I have blest thee --

Ye shall now give unto them this Word - and it shall be unto them which receive it - much Light --

= The Way =

There is but One Way unto Mine Father's House - that is thru Me - for I Am He which is set over the Gate - thru which they must enter -- There are no rogues within this place of Mine Abode - they enter not by the side road - they enter not thru the back roads - neither thru the underground --

= The Anointing =

I say: They come by the hi-road - the strait and narrow - they walk the hi-road with perfect sureness - they faint not - neither do they fail --

I say: They come by the Gate which now stands ajar - and I am the Gate Keeper - I am the Overseer -- I know them by their light - I know them by name - and number - - and when they approach Me - I call their name - and they shall answer: "Here I am" "HERE - AM I"- and they shall be as ones blest to hear their name called - and they shall answer --

= Sweet Perfume =

When it is come that they hear their name called - they shall be unafraid to answer - for they shall Know Mine Voice - and answer with assurance that I am nigh -- So be it that I shall bless them - and I shall anoint them with the Oil and Balm sweet - and they shall find comfort and their strength shall be sufficient unto the day thereof -- For the show goes on - and the business at hand shall be as a sweetness they have not known before - for it shall be as the dew unto the rose - as perfume unto the olfactory nerve - as the color of the rose to the eye - - for it shall give unto them joy - and they shall serve Me with Great joy. And a heartfelt Gladness shall be as a Sweet Vial - and they shall know that they have been blest --

= Associates =

I say they shall serve Me gladly - for I make no "slaves" of Mine servants - - they are Mine Associates - Mine Fellow-Brothers - - and I ask not of them that which I would not do - that which they cannot do.

They shall be clad in the raiment of flesh - and they shall know that I am with them - and that I am One which hast walked the same Way in which I bid them come -- I <u>Know</u> each step of the Way - - I have walked it with measured step - - I have been unto My calling true - - I ask of them no less - for - as I have been this way before them - I Know the Victory which shall crown the Victor - and the Joy of attaining --

So be it I say: Hail! Hail unto the Victor! For he has <u>won</u> his Victory!

None other hast won it for him - - He alone hast earned it - so be it the law -- So shall it ever be -- Amen - and Selah --

= To the Recorder =

Sori Sori -- This I would say unto thee this day: Be ye as one blest to give this Mine Word unto them - and they shall profit to receive it - for it is for their good that I give it unto them - - they shall receive it - or reject it -- It is for their own sake that I lower Mine Light that I come into their midst at this time --

= The Heedless =

Now it is come when they shall be found wanting - they stand in need and I come Crying unto them to Awaken - and few there be which have answered Me - - I say; Few - there be - which hast answered Mine call.

= The Search =

I have cried unto them in a loud Voice - and they have turned unto their false gods - their soothsayers - their necromancers - and magicians - - they have taken unto the mountains and the seas - in search of peace - knowing not where peace is to be found --

I say: They know not that peace is to be found within their own heart -- They cry for peace - yet - they look unto another for peace -- wherein they find only confusion and disappointment --

They summons the couriers and the lawmakers - they summons their bishop - and priests - that they might bring forth the peace from the chaos - and wherein have they found peace?

= Confusion =

Peace is within the Realm of Light - yet they have not the Light - neither the Wisdom to bring Peace out of chaos -- The chaos is of their own making - - they have taken from the "Word of God"- and added unto - they have misrepresented the "Word" - - they have put upon it their own interpretations - - they have multiplied their "Sins" and compounded them! - yea - they have compounded them a thousand times - and now they shall compute them - and they shall find that they are none the wiser --

They shall stand in fear and trembling of their own creations - for they have created without reckoning - - they have created their own monsters - which lie in wait to devour them -- They shall be as ones swallowed up by their own creations -- They shall stand in want/ in fear/ and be as the foolish crying - help! help! - For indeed they shall be as ones helpless --

= Redemption Draweth Nigh =

They shall be as ones blest to turn unto Me - and bring unto Me their heart - their hands - their wills - and serve Me with all their strength - - and then - I shall bless them - and give unto them succor - and bring them out of their plight --

This is Mine part - to deliver them from their own pit - which they have prepared for themself -- They know not that they have betrayed themself - they have thot themself wise - - they have been as the blind leading the blind--

Now I speak unto them which have the mind to follow Me - that they might be prepared to go where I go -- So be it that I am the Way - the Truth - the Light -- I fashion for them no pits - no legirons - - I fashion for them no snares - no traps - yet - I know that which is prepared for them -- All the pitfalls - snares - traps - - these are the tools of the dark one - the Prince of Darkness --

So be it I point the way - - I bring the Light which I Am - I come bringing Justice and Mercy for All - and no man shall set up a barrier that I cannot cross --

= Love Knows No Barrier =

I say: No barrier is sufficient to stay Mine hand -- Yet - they which set foot against Me - shall fall and be as nothing unto Me - for I am not to be denied - I come to find Mine own - I come to deliver up Mine own.

It is said: "Seek ye the Light which I Am - and I shall find thee"-- So be it and Selah --

= The Lodestone =

They shall seek Me out - and they shall be blest -- I bring them not against their will - I say - they come of their own accord -- They shall be as ones prepared to go where I go - and none other shall enter in - for I go unto Mine Father which hast Sent Me - and they shall be as ones blest to go with Me --

= The Text =

"Prepare thyself!"- shall be Mine Theme Song unto them which have asked for Light -- "Prepare! Prepare! <u>Prepare for thy Victory</u>!"- shall be My Text - for this is Mine Preachments -- For the time comes swiftly when I shall send forth Mine Couriers in Great numbers - that they awaken - - and they shall go forth as in a Great Troop - as a Great Army and none shall be found without light*-- While the light may be overshadowed - or placed under a scarf - it shall be seen - and fanned - and made brighter --

For that matter - it shall be the beginning of a greater work - Greater than anything done since man first began his journey upon Earth -- I say - this is the Greatest Work begun - since man first walked the

Earth** - for it is the Greater Part -- And he slumbers while "We of the Host" go forward - that We be as the Hand of God The Father --

And I speak of the <u>Power</u> of The <u>Almighty</u> Father The One Which hast brot forth the Plan - the Creation of the Universe, the Universes untold/ unnumbered - and peopled them - and given of Himself that there be Life/ Light -- So be it that He shall be unto them ALL that He hast promised - - He shall be unto Himself true - - and HE NEVER FAILS!!

= The Father's Will =

So be it that I Am His Will - made manifest - and I Am the Living Will, the Hand of Him Which is the Cause of Mine Being - the Heart beat - the Pulse of Him Which hast Sent Me --

Bear ye witness of Me - and be ye as one prepared to return with Me - and ye shall know as I Know -- Then - We shall sing together the Praise - and the Glory - which shall be Our Anthem unto His Mercy - and His Love - - and Peace shall abide forever with Us -- Holy - Holy Holy - is the Name of Solen Aum Solen - let thy Voice be Mine and ye shall Know Him as I Know Him -- So be it and Selah --

= Instructions =

Place this Mine Word with the latter part of that which ye have just finished - and it shall be for the ones which have the foregoing parts - which has been completed - and this shall begin the next part - which shall be as a book - separate from the part preceding this --

= Responsibility of the Recorder =

Matters not if it is given in parts/ "portions"- or in book form - for they shall be as ones which has been given the "Word" - and then - they shall be responsible for that which they do with it -- Herein ends thy own responsibility -- Bear ye in mind - it is thy responsibility to give it unto them - therein ends thy responsibility - for I shall not hold thee responsible for that which they do with "the Word" -- Yet - it shall be understood - that they which put underfoot the Word of God - shall be brot to account for their foolishness - and they shall be as ones which have betrayed themself - and their trust --

*"By thy light art thou found"

**"Coming - the Greatest Show on Earth"

= To the Ones Who Receive =

So be it - it behooves Me to say: "Be aware of the Word - the Work - the Service which is rendered thee this day" --

Be ye as ones prepared for the Greater Part which is kept for thee - So be it ye shall earn thy Victory - and it shall be according unto the law --

I say: "SEE YE THE HAND OF GOD MOVE! SEE IT MOVE!" Hear ye the Voice - Calling: Come - Come ye forth - and prepare thyself for to receive Me - for I AM COME - I AM COME - - Bear ye witness of Me - and rejoice with Me --

So let it be a Glad Day - and together we shall rejoice for thy deliverance!

So let it be - as The Father hast Willed it --

Amen and Selah --

Recorded by Sister Thedra

This I would have Known

Sori Sori -- Be ye as one prepared for that which I say unto thee - for it shall be as part of the record -- It shall go in the record as part of the permanent record - and for them which are to come after thee --

= This I would have Known =

They which do Mine Work are Mine Servants - Mine Chosen - for these are valuable in Mine Work - - without these I cannot do Mine Work --

For these are Mine Hand Maiden - thru which I accomplish Mine Work -- I am the Director - I am the Word - I am the Inspirator - I Am the Will - I am He which hast Sent thee forth that Mine Will be done on Earth as it is in Heaven -- So be it that I have established this House and I have set thee over it - even as I am set over the House of God - and which hast within it Many houses - departments - Many Mansions.

= Inadequacy of Words =

These are but <u>words</u> which are designed to convey unto thee the fullness of the Plan -- Yet - I say: No pen can put the fullness on paper.

No tongue - in any language - can convey unto thee one iota of the vastness of the "Great and Divine Plan - of which ye are but part!"

I say: Each part is essential - and important unto the WHOLE -- Whereby I say: Be ye as one responsible for thy part - and unto the responsible - greater responsibility is given -- So be it and Selah --

Now the time comes swiftly - when ye shall stand within the place wherein I am - and ye shall see that which hast been accomplished -- So be it and Selah --

Ye shall bear witness of Me - and ye shall stand with Me - and ye shall serve Me WELL - for I say unto thee: I Am the Light of the World I Am the Life - and the Way -- So be it that ye shall Know as I Know - for all things shall be revealed unto thee --

Ye shall be as one blest of Me - and ye shall stand and see the Glory of The Father -- Ye shall be as one Glorified and blest - as I have been blest --

Rest assured that I know that which I say unto thee - and ye shall be as one on whose head shall rest the Crown of Victory -- So be it - and Selah --

Now ye shall place this within the place which is designed for it - and it shall follow the last part - which was designed for the next book Omit the one which was spoken at the hour of three - before sunrise - for it was for thine own eyes - and none other -- Place this one in the book - which is to follow the "Papa Papers"-- This Mine note - shall also be included - for I am He which hast the foresight which supersedes thine own -- Be ye blest to receive the forthcoming parts - and ye shall do well -- So be it and Selah --

= The Host =

Sori Sori -- Blest be this day - blest be those who come into this House for I the Lord God hast brot forth this House - I have set up Mine Altar in the midst thereof - and I have put into thy hands Mine Word - Mine Sayings - and thou hast given unto Me thy time and energy - thy loyalty and I shall not forget thee in the time of trial - - for I have said unto thee: I am thy Shield and thy Buckler - and I shall be unto thee all the Father would have Me be -- I say unto thee: Be ye as one blest of Me and by Me - and give unto them as ye have received - and ye shall be blest as I have been blest -- So be it and Selah --

Give unto them which come unto thee - this Word - and they shall profit by their acceptance of it -- So be it I am prepared to do Mine part so let it profit them to accept the Word - - for this is it given --

Amen and Selah --

= The Builder & The Piper =

Sori Sori -- For this part let it be added unto the last - and it shall be as part of the book now being prepared - to be given unto them in parts or portions --

This I would have them Know - that the ones which apply the Word unto themselves - and which take it unto themselves - and fashion for themself the Greater part - shall be as ones blest -- Yet - the ones which read - and lay aside that which they have read - and that which hast been unto them as so much paper - so much ink - - these shall be as ones which have not seen - not heard - not known that which is said - neither that which goes on in front of their face --

For they are blind - deaf - and will not know that which goes on before their eyes --

= To the Foolish =

I say: - They simply have not prepared themself for to see - and they shall not know that which is being done -- While they have the Key within their hand - they have not found it - - they have not prepared themself for to use it - they are like unto a babe which holds the "Key" and knows not the purpose thereof - neither does he have the stature to reach the latch --

I say: The Key hast been placed within their hand - and they have not found it -- These put aside the "Paper" as so many words - they have simply read words - and have not found the meaning thereof - - they have not seen that which hast been said - neither shall they see that which is being done -- They shall come - and go - as they come - knowing not that which goes on - for they have not prepared themself for to see - hear - and to know --

= The Piper =

Now it is given unto Me to say: They shall be as ones wanting - as ones WAITING!

They shall wait - and want - - for they shall be as ones which have been the lookers - and have not seen -- These shall be as the ones opinionated - they shall be as the ones which have not seen - for their opinions and preconceived ideas have been unto them a trap - - they - have thot themself wise - while they have been enmeshed within their own trap -- They have come unto the "Feast" - with their bellies full - and they have not partaken of the Food which hast been placed before them -- They have dined sumptuously on the chaff - which shall be unto them much bulk - no nourishment --

They shall be as ones bloated and distressed - and find that they have hungered - and put that which hast been unto them Great Anguish within their stomachs - and rejected that which would have been unto them Great Nourishment - Strength - and Delight - leaving in them Great Peace - and Well Being --

= The Foolish =

These I call the foolish - they THINK themself wise - they put their hands in their pocket and pay the piper for his "Merry tune" - and they turn a deaf ear unto the cry for help - from the Servants which I send forth to deliver them out of bondage --

I SAY:

"They pay the piper for his merry tune - and deny Mine Servants - which spreads before them the banquet table"--

I CALL THEM:

Unto the Feast - - I call them - and they follow the Merry Piper - - they dance unto his tune - - they follow gladly - and he leads them down into the shadows - and deserts them - - wherein they find themself lost and the magic of the tune gone -- They fear - and cry out - yet he hast left them on their own - forsaken - and lost -- They wander - and wonder and they find they have been betrayed - they have danced to the foolish piper - and he hast DESERTED THEM!!

= Watch for Traps! =

They shall cry out in their sorrow: Help! Help! - and they shall cry as the lost child -- They shall find that they shall be heard - and they shall find that they have been as ones which have the "Free will" - the Gift given of the Father - - they have used it to follow the piper - now they shall use it to follow the "Way Shower" - which is in the other direction which is unto the Light - which is unto the hilands - the uproad - and wherein there are no traps --

= Personal Action =

I say - they shall first <u>Seek</u> the Light - they shall put forth their left foot then their right foot - and they shall step forth and make the effort of their own accord -- They shall find that I shall go forth to meet them with outstretched arms - and I shall be unto them all the Father would have Me be -- I shall be unto them the Comforter - the Shield and Buckler - the Rod and the Staff - and they shall follow Me - and they shall find that I shall lead them out of their bondage and confusion -- They shall be as ones free to go where I go - and they shall go <u>freely</u> - they shall come freely - and none shall say unto them NAY! None shall say unto them Stay!

= Tools or Toys? =

So be it I have said: Come! - and they shall come of their own free will or they shall wait -- So be it I am not hurried - neither am I a piper -- I give not that which comforts them in their conceit -- I bring not toys for the foolish - I bring tools - for the adults -- I bring food for the "little child" which cries for bread --

I bring forth <u>Substance</u> that the humble be sustained - - I bring forth Nourishment - and I Know which is which!!

= **The Master Builder** =

I say:

The foolish ask for foolish things - the wise ask for tools - that they might build yet greater -- So be it I am a builder - I build Greater - I build upon the ROCK - I build that the winds do not destroy --

I build not of card - or straw -

I build of Steadier Stuff -

I choose Mine tools -

I choose My building material -

I build unto Eternal things -

I waste not Mine Substance -

I bring forth beauty out of chaos -

I bring perfection out of ugliness -

I bring joy out of sorrow -

I bring Majesty out of lowliness -

I bring Sympathy out of intolerance -

I bring activity out of apathy -

I bring Fortitude out of dreariness -

I bring humbleness out of bigotry -

I bring Strength out of weakness -

I bring Courage out of despair - and Light out of darkness -- for this am I Sent --

I Say:

I Come in Strength -

I Come in Power -

I Come in Love -

I Come in Wisdom -

I Come in Compassion -

I Come in the Light -

I Come in Great Numbers -

I Come in Joy - and in the Fortress of Mine Father's Love and Will I Come with the Mighty Host - with the Power and Glory of an Exalted Host -- I stand ever ready to assist a hungry - befuddled people - a world atotter - a world berserk - a world afrighted - a world astride the chasm of despair - a world divided - a world adrift!

I Say:

I Am Come - I Am Come! - and I stand ready to assist - for I am come that they be brot out of darkness - - for this Am I Sent -- So let it be as The Father hast Willed it -- This I would say unto them which have the will to follow Me:

There is but little time that ye have - before ye are called into the Realms wherein ye shall abide for a time* - and ye shall now prepare thy abiding place - for as ye prepare thyself - so shall ye receive - - for the physician shall find his place prepared for him - the carpenter shall be in his own place - the farmer shall till his fields - the mason shall build yet Greater mansions - the piper shall find his pipes - the laggard shall find his pallet hard - and the vendor shall find his viands - - each unto his own environment - and none shall be out of place --

I SAY:

Prepare thyself - for Greater things than "these" shall ye do -- These are but the tinker's toys - - prepare thyself for the tools of the wise -- Accept that which I offer thee - and it shall suffice thee that I Am Come that ye be prepared for the Greater Part -- So be it and Selah --

*ref G. Vale Owen books:

Rolf's life in the Spirit World

= The Overflow =

Sori Sori -- Now I speak as One faithful unto Mine trust -- I speak as One prepared to give unto thee that which I have kept for thee -- I say I have kept the Goodly part - and ye shall partake of it in portions - for thou couldst not take all thine Goodly part at one time - for it wouldst overcome thee - thou couldst not bear it -- Yet - ye shall partake of the fullness of thine inheritance when thine time is come -- So be it that the time approaches swiftly when ye shall stand with Me - and drink from Mine Cup - and ye shall fill thine own from Mine Cup - and in turn ye shall fill the Cup of a multitude from the overflow of thine Cup - which thou hast received from Mine -- So be it and Selah --

= The Light =

Sori Sori -- I say: I AM - and for that thou Art - - I AM - and for that - Art thou -- Therein is the mystery of thy being - - yet - I have said unto thee: "Ye shall come to Know as I Know"- and ye shall find that all mysteries have their ending in Me - for I Am the Light and the WAY - I Am He which hast brot thee hence - and I shall bring thee forth as a living witness of the WORD -- I place upon thee a Holy Benediction - and it shall sustain thee - and ye shall Know Me - and ye shall partake of Mine Substance - and there shall be no want - for I shall be sufficient unto thee - and ye shall dwell in the House of the Lord forever -- So be it and Selah --

Place thine hand in Mine - and I shall lead thee into the paths of Righteousness - and We shall rejoice together - and ye shall say with Me: Praise! Praise! unto the Father of Heaven and Earth - for He hast brot forth His Sons and Daughters - He hast brot forth His Harvest - and He hast been as One Glorified in them -- He hast risen them above the beast-hood - and He hast Graced His Household by their presence for they have become His Children by adoption - and they have claimed Him Father of All - for His is the Glory and the Power forever and forever -- So be it and Selah -- I Am His Will made manifest -- So be it and Selah –

* * *

= Guests =

Sori Sori -- Be ye blest this day - and give unto thyself the rest and quiet necessary for that which ye are to do -- Be ye as one prepared for the work at hand - and know ye thine time is Mine time --

Close thy door - and sit not with them which would usurp thy time for it profits thee not --

Hold thyself in readiness - and fortune thyself the Greater part - - for it is given unto Me to see thee engaged in trivialities - which accrue no profit --

So let it be that I shall steady thine hand - and I shall place upon thy hearth a log which shall burn brightly - and they shall warm themself thereby -- Yet - they shall be profited to be as the guest within Mine House - for they shall come into Mine House as Mine Guest - as I am the Host - and I know them and their needs --

Yet - I say: There are ones which have not the good manners to abide by Mine laws - Mine Word - and they have misused thee -- and their lodging hast defiled Mine House - for they have come as directed yet they have brot with them their own opinions - and bigotry -- They have been unprepared to accept that which I have for them - they forfeit the prize I have proffered them - they have accepted the lesser part --

Now ye shall be as one separate and apart from the ones which would defile the House of the Lord - and which would be unto thee a wayward child --

I say: There are none so foolish as the one which thinks himself wise -- So be it and Selah --

Now ye shall be as one apart - and let it suffice that I am with thee and I am thy Friend - thy Counselor - and thy Shield and thy Buckler - So be it I am the Wayshower - and I am not to be turned out of Mine House -- So be it I am come that ye be about the Father's Business - - let it be - let it be - let it be --

So shall I prepare before thee a table - and ye shall eat and be nourished and satisfied -- So be ye blest to partake of Mine Substance for I am come that ye be sustained -- So be it - and Selah --

Let <u>thine</u> <u>time</u> <u>be</u> <u>Mine</u> <u>time</u> - and I shall bless thee - and ye shall not want -- So be it and Selah --

How do I rightly interpret this Lord - do I go to altar this am? T.

Yes - and thereafter ye shall have thine time for a "cup"* - and thereafter make thine way into thy own sanctuary - and be as one prepared to receive Me - and of Me - for I shall give unto thee a part for the book which is being prepared -- Ye shall not let them which are no part of thy household deter thee from the work at hand - for it is fortuned unto Me to see them as ones unprepared - and of no value in Mine House -- They enter not into Mine place of abode unprepared - therefore I say: "Prepare - Prepare - Prepare"- and they come <u>seeking</u> - What? They bring with them their own puny parts - and they hear not that which I say --

I say unto thee:

Close thy door - and give unto Me thine time - and it shall profit thee -- So be it and Selah --

= For the Communication =

Sori Sori -- <u>Hear ye Me this day</u> - and be ye alert -- Fashion for thyself a place wherein ye might be alone with Me - that ye might be in silence and wherein there shall be no interruptions - for I shall be as One prepared to give unto thee a part which is new - and different - and ye shall be the one to prepare thyself to receive it --

There shall be no interruptions - no place shall ye be wherein they shall come or call thee - for it shall be done in silence - and without any disturbance -- So be it We shall begin this day -- After thy Altar Service is finished – ye shall return unto the chosen place - and make ready thyself for thy part - it shall profit thee -- So be it and Selah --

*Breakfast drink with the guest

= The Author =

Point out to them that they shall assist thee in this - and give unto them this Mine Word - and let it suffice that I am the Author of these Mine Words - and they shall accept them in Mine name - for I Know that which I am about - I KNOW! I am the Author and the Finisher of Mine Work - and I say: I have begun a Greater Work than they have imaged. So let it be known that ye are about the Father's Business -- So be it I have called thee - and ye have answered Me -- Now We shall go forth as One - and We shall do that which is given unto Us of The Father -- So be it and Selah --

= Fortune thyself the Greater Part =

Let not thy hand slip - for ye shall be as one on whose shoulders rests great responsibility - and ye shall be true unto thy trust - - and not one letter shall be out of place - not one word shall be changed -- So be it that I have given unto thee thy Gift - and it shall profit thee to use it and be unto Me Mine Handmaiden - Mine Voice unto them which have a mind to learn of Me - - for this have I called thee forth -- So be it and Selah --

Now ye shall go unto them - and read that which I have said unto another Servant - now with Me - - and he shall be as one prepared to give unto thee a part -- He - shall be as one prepared to speak in Mine name - and he shall do a Mighty Work - and none shall deny him his speech - for he shall speak freely - - for he is one of the Goodly Crowd, the Goodly Company -- I say: He is one prepared to speak - and ye shall receive him as ye have received Me -- So be it and Selah --

Recorded by Sister Thedra

= Keep Mine Commandments =

Blest are they which obey the law -- Blest are they which keep the way unto Mine House - for they shall abide in the House of the Lord forever and they shall be blest as I have been blest -- For this I have bidden thee Come - for this have I placed Mine Seal upon thee - - for thou hast kept the Commandments of the Lord - and it is given unto thee to be the one appointed the task of giving forth this Word - - as it is given - so shall ye give it - and no word shall be changed --

For it shall be as it is - it shall be presented unto them in such manner as I present it unto thee -- Ye shall not embellish the Word - neither shall ye take from it one iota --

For it shall be sufficient unto itself -- The Word shall need no embellishment - it shall need no pruning or shearing - it shall be as I have seen fit to give it -

For I Know that which I am about --

So be it ye shall now receive of this one which hast prepared himself for this part -- He hast long awaited this hour - when he might speak out unto them which have the will to receive that which he has for them --

He brings much Light - Strength - and Wisdom --

He hast appointed himself this part - for his preparation hast been long and strenuous - and he hast complied with the law -- Now he stands approved by the Great and Mighty Council - his passport is approved - therefore he cometh thru and by the consent of the Council and I stand with him - as I am the Doorkeeper - I give him admittance Receive him in Mine name - - so be it I give unto him the Power and Authority to speak --

Blest am I - blest are We - that this be given unto Us - that they might come to know the Power which is invested within the Spirit of Man - by the Grace of Our Father - which hast given unto Us being --

Let it be known that I am not far removed from the earthly scenes - I am with them which labor in the field - that men of Earth be brot out of their ignorance -- The ignorance of man is appalling unto us when we have gained the heights - when we have turned to look upon the scenes below --

= Higher Ground =

I say: "The Scenes below"- for I say: We have been brot unto Higher Ground - therefore we see with the Greater Vision - - we see as without the veil - the "colored glasses" - we see with vision clear --

I am now prepared to speak unto them which have ears to hear - and the will to learn --

= Lower Ground =

This I would say: There is but few who are of a mind to hear or to learn they are as ones entranced with their own burdens - their own political views - and puny positions and theories --

Yet I say for a certainty - that they will lay aside all their pettiness ere they come into the place wherein I am --

This I would say unto them which have the will to free themself from the net of devilishness - which they have so meticulously woven for themselves: - Put aside the smallness of thy puny will - thy pride - thy preconceived ideas of the "Christ" - the Heavens - the Hells - and the Saints - the Man called "Jesus" - - and turn unto the Light -- Ask nought of man - neither search ye the records for Light - for it is not contained within books -- Neither is man given unto seeking Light - - he is given unto searching for that which man hast brot forth - which will verify his own opinions - and give unto him comfort --

In his ignorance he hast departed from the Light - which hast brot forth all the Great Artists - Scientists - and Masters of the Law -- They have been as children looking for their toys - - and when they are found they tire of them - and cast them aside for another day --

= To the Few =

There be few who are now prepared to step forth and declare themselves. While it is said: "There be few" - it is seen that "the few" shall be leaders of men - and they shall stand firm - and be as ones prepared to lead them thru the flames -- For I say unto thee: The children shall be tried as by fire! - they shall not escape!!

Now ye shall be as one which hast gone forth as by a Mighty Calling - and ye shall be blest to be among the few which shall stand - and ye shall confront the oppressors - and the tormentors - - they shall surge against thee - and they shall be as the oppressors -- The forces of darkness shall overrun the land - and they shall be as the black hoard - as the pestilence which go forth to destroy --

= Watchword =

The Watchword is: "Stand ye firm"! Watch! See! Know that which goes on about thee --

= Hold Thy Tongue! =

Be ye circumspect - wait upon the Lord - serve Him - in thy service unto man - for without Him there is no hope --

Know ye that there is a Host which stands ready to assist - - yet it cometh upon a world asleep - - when they shall be found without the proper necessities to withstand the enemy - for he neither gives them the help - the warning - nor the courtesy of their forerunners - to enlighten them of their plans -- They send before them no summons to battle - - they creep up in the shadows - to make mischief and do deviltry while they sleep --

= The Dead =

Asleep? - they are as dead!! - I say: They are dead on their feet!

They are not alert - they are not aware - they are as robots - animated by that which they know not --

They neither know which they have done - or that which they are to do --

They go about as a machine - operated by a coin -- They have but to stand still - and see that which goes on about them --

They question not the time - the day - the hour -- They know not that the hour swiftly approaches when they shall cry for Our assistance. They shall cry long - and loud! - therefore it behooves Us here in this place - upon this "Higher Ground" - to be alert unto the day - the hour when the cry for help goes up - - and then We shall come in and give our assistance - as We find wise and expedient --

It is with Great heartfelt delight - Soul Delight - that I am privileged to speak with thee - and I shall put within thy hand the part which I have been preparing for them which have awaited the Word from Me - and the Word shall be as Mine - and none others - for I shall take full responsibility for that which I say --

Ye shall have no fear of thy part - for it shall be as thy part - - and Mine shall be Mine - each assuming full responsibility thereof -- So be it none shall set foot against thee - for that which I do or say -- Ye shall rest assured that thy protection is complete -- So be it that the Mighty Host stands watch - to secure thy position - and to assure thy passage into the place wherein I am -- So be it and Selah --

Place thine foot upon higher Ground - and ye shall be as one of the Host -- Let thine protection be as Mine - and ye shall FEAR NOT - for ten thousand shall fall before thee - ten thousand shall fall behind thee ten thousand shall fall at thy right - ten thousand at thy left - but I say - ye shall not fall - for the Host is with thee - and thy passage is assured thee -- So be it thy passport is in order -- So let it be - as the Father hast Willed it --

I shall speak at a later hour -- Ye shall now rest - and refresh thyself and I shall speak unto thee of things to come --

= Sons of God and Bastards =

Par - and par - shall be the time - and half time - for the half time shall equal the time - - yet the half time shall be as the hour - and the time shall be as the day - yet the hour shall equal the day --

Now ye shall see the hour as ye saw the day - it shall pass and leave its renderings -- It shall shape men's destinies - and the future of generations yet unborn--

For the recording of time is written in men's blood - - and the scavengers shall clean the bones - and the fields shall be enriched by the carnage -- And yet men shall dwell within the lowlands - and they shall drink of the pollution from the carnage - and they shall be polluted thereby --

Know ye that men are not all born of Kings - not all know the Kingdom of the Righteous - not all have the Sonship - granted unto them which are born of the King --

Not all are of Royal Birth - for some are bastards - some of low birth - begotten of Satan - - and wherein is it said: "<u>they</u> are soulless"--

For not all are Sons of the Living God -- The Father Solen Aum Solen Created ALL that is created - GOOD - He Created Wisely - and GOOD --

Now be ye as one alert - and feign not privily - that ye have the knowledge of that which I say - for it is given unto Me to see them shrug and say: "O - yes - I Know" - and yet they have not known - they have thot these Words Symbolmatic - they have thot them as so many words - conveying No Truth - -

Yet - I say: These which are bastards have no father save Satan - for he hast created them - and breathed into them life - yet they are as robots - - soulless art they - for he - Satan - has not the power to create within the souls - therefore such are "bastards" - they are not of the Eternal - - they are as the breeze - and shall pass and be no more -- So be it that I shall tell thee of these at a future time --

Let it suffice that they come that they make mischief - that they torment the opposite - the ones which are of Light -- And it is given unto Me to see them as mischief-makers - - they persecute - ridicule - and annoy the ones which are called to do the Father's Will -- They are as the ones sent forth from the pit - for to do the will of the dark one - and he hast endowed unto them life of his life - and he animates his creation - and sends it forth as ones in flesh - and it is given unto man to accept them as '"man" - for he sees not the underside of him - and the blackness within him --

He hast the head liken unto man - he walks liken unto man - yet he hast within his bosom the heart of the beast - and he knows not from whence he came - neither does he claim relationship with his source - for he knows not his father --

Born of Satan is he - therefore he shall be cast into utter darkness - and be <u>no</u> more - for he is not of Eternal variety -- he shall pass and be no more seen of men -- So be it and Selah --

Now ye shall rest and return - and I shall speak again --

= Help of the Wise =

This I would give unto thee - and for this hour is it given -- The time is upon us when we gather at the River - - for as a Mighty Army We stand ready to go out - and we do go in pairs - in great mass - as is expedient We go into the world of man - and we do that which is assigned unto us -- We have been assigned Special Missions - such as entering into the affairs of men - for the purpose of directing them aright - for giving unto them greater insight into the baffling problems which befront them.

We give unto their problems serious consideration - and seek the solution from our vantage point --

We give unto them counsel - and pay unto them their due - when it is come that they have earned the right to our assistance --

I say - many cry out for help - and for selfish reasons - - these are not answered in their kind - for we are not slaves unto their selfish desires - we give not of our energy - our time - unto the ones which call for self alone --

For we have seen the selfish man cry out for help - that he enslave his brother - his neighbor and his servant--

We give unto him no alms - that he imprison the impoverished --

We wait - and wait - until he has gained by his own lessons - the wisdom to seek help for the whole of mankind - for all - that the Whole be lifted up --

There is Wisdom in our waiting -- There is Justice in our waiting - There is no justice in aiding and abetting the injustice of man --

They shall learn that Justice is the fruit of honest labor - and Love is the fruit which crowns the head of the Victor - - for his garlands shall be woven by his own hands - and he shall wear the garlands which he weaves for himself -- They shall pierce the head of the unjust man - and he shall weary of his own "laurel crown"- for the crown shall pierce his brow - even as his heel pierced the flesh of his brother which he hast enslaved --

Pity is the man which gives unto his brother the leaden penny for his honest labor --

Pity is the man which withholds the wage earned --

Pity is the man which takes from his brother the wage earned -- Wherein is it said: "A man is withal - his brother's keeper"? And has he dealt justly with him? Has he been unto him a brother? Hast he given unto him the leaden penny for his days labor? Or put his finger on the scales for the ounce of flesh?

Wherein hast he cut the ounce?

Wherein hast he added rocks unto the flour?

Wherein hast he put the nails in the bag of wheat - that it weigh the heavier?

I say - it is not according unto the law - to assist them which have no thot of their fellow man --

They pray: "O - Lord Help Me!" - Wherein have they helped?

I say their prayers carry a stench - which is foul in our nostrils!

We see the blackness of their desires -- their thots are to deceive and to destroy --

= Karma =

They froth at the mouth as dogs gone mad - and pit their wits against the brother -- and their heads are as mallets - they beat them into the wall - and they reason not that they are forging their own legirons - their own stanchions --

They reason not - that they are forging the weapons of destruction whereby they be destroyed --

Let them reason - let them look - let them see the folly of their way And they shall profit to turn from their own folly - and give unto his fellow brothers the benefit of his energy - and his assistance - that they be as one - - and in unity they shall bring forth a New Nation - and a New Generation shall be born - which will benefit by his effort --

This shall the coming generation inherit = <u>that</u> <u>which</u> <u>man</u> <u>now</u> <u>gives</u> <u>unto</u> <u>it</u> - as their legacy - their inheritance - and none shall stay the hand of fortune --

It is said: "The sins of the Nation shall be inherited by the coming generations"- and it is true - for are the fathers of the next generation not now in flesh?

Are they not now sowing the seed for their offspring?

Man - what art thou sowing for the future generation - which ye shall be the father to - of - and responsible for? Pay ye heed! I pray ye heed ere ye fall into the pit - for it is no fallacy - it is no idle admonition the pit is gaping wide - and wherein many are entrapt --

I say ye shall take heed this day - and counsel shall be given ere you slip into the pit -- It is the law ye be warned - it is given that ye be warned - - but NO LAW says: Ye <u>have</u> to heed it!

Take it or leave it - as ye choose - it is thine choice --

We of the Host speak that ye fall not - yet we speak for the Good of All - not for one alone -- While we see All of mankind as One - We know that there are many - many - minds - many personalities - and diverse opinions - and yet these are but parts of the Whole - - they are not as the ones aware of the Whole - while in flesh - yet when they see from the Greater heights - they shall see themself as part of One Great Family - of "Humanity"--

We are but part of the Whole - yet we stand on higher ground - as the enlightened ones we stand - Knowing as they know not -- Therefore

We stoop - we bend - both head - back - and <u>Know</u> we bend - - We lift a hand to help - to bless - to assist in their ascent --

We give all - ask nought - we Know the blessing of giving -- We ask nought but to give unto them which are prepared to receive - - yet the Sun is made to shine on the just and unjust alike -- So be it that we give of our love - and it goes forth that All be blest - yet not all accept it - for they are not as ones alert unto Us - - of Our going and coming they are not aware - - they are as ones troubled with their own puny problems - details of small things - and they fear the part which we would reveal unto them - for they have been indoctrinated with fear -- It is said - they serve the dragon fearlessly - while they fear the Light - for he the dragon whispers sweet warnings in their ear: "<u>Fear this</u> - <u>for it is unknown unto thee</u> - - <u>watch</u>! <u>ye know the part which he gives unto thee is new</u> - <u>untried</u> - <u>unpopular</u> - <u>and ye should be unpopular with thy associates</u> - <u>they would make of thee a thing of ridicule</u> - <u>if you should speak of these things</u> - - <u>prove these things first</u> - <u>and accept them later</u>".

Wherein is it said: "Seek ye the Light - seek - and ye shall find"- -

It is so - - ye shall seek and ye accept that which is proffered - in Light - Love - and Wisdom --

Ye walk by faith - for it is by faith that ye ask - by faith that ye live by faith that ye walk in righteousness - - then ye shall receive thine inheritance - because thou hast walked in the way of righteousness - knowing not thine reward -- It is for righteousness sake - that ye follow in "His footsteps" - it is for the love of righteousness that ye become righteous -- So be it and Selah -- Rest -

= Peace and / or War =

There are rumors of Peace - - where are there rumors of Peace? Where are there rumors of Peace?

Within the halls of Congress?

Within the halls of Parliaments?

Within the Council Chambers?

Yea - even in the low places wherein dwells the peasant - he hast heard the <u>rumors</u> of peace - yet he knoweth of War -- War hast he had for that matter - hast he known else?

Wherein hast he not had war within his own house? Wherein hast he been at peace within his own household?

I am but One of a Mighty Host - which is brot forth that war might cease - that peace profound be established -- I say: Peace is first established upon thine own hearth - and within thine own household --

So be it that I am speaking unto the Man on whose shoulders rests the responsibility of his own salvation - for he alone is his own Savior. He alone shall make his bed - he shall lie within the bed which he makes for himself - for it is said - he is responsible unto none other for his own torment -- He shall arise and come forth - or he shall faint by the way - He shall either bring himself of his own accord - or reject the hand so lovingly proffered him --

Fain would I give unto him that which would deter his progress - -

Yet joyfully would I give My All to assist him in his ascent - for do I not know the climb to be torturous and wearing -- I say it is not the easy way - yet it is the safe and sure way - for at the end the Victory won - never to be lost - Never - No Never!

Place before them this Mine Word - and I shall speak again of Greater things - and ye shall receive of Me that which I have prepared for thee -- Raise on the morrow - and await Mine coming - and I shall portray for thee a play which hast begun - and it shall be as the last play of the season - for many shall gather within the Arena - to view the Scenes being enacted by the players --

It happens that I am but One -- So be it that thou hast a part - not unlike Mine - yet different - inasmuch as ye are there - I am here - yet it is made clearer unto Me - Mine Part -- Ye see as thru a dark screen - the curtain is heavy - and the stage is dark - - while the light shall gleam brighter and brighter as the play goes on -- So be it the Play goes on --

So be it We are Participants - - wait -

Recorded by Sister Thedra

= A Sweet Sonnet I Bring Beloved =

So be it that I speak unto thee in tongue sweet - in music unto thy soul in the rhythm of thine heart -- I bequeath unto thee a sweet song - I bring unto thee a sonnet - - sing it in the morn - sing it at noon day - sing it in the eventide - sing it at the midnite hour --

Let it ring forth that they might know the sweetness - that they bear witness of Me in the stillness of the night - in the rush of the noon hour.

Bring forth the sweetness of the morn - that they be refreshed -- As the day bringeth its toil - its shadows - its pain and woe - I say: Bring forth the sweetness of Mine Sonnet - which I place upon thy lips --

Praise ye the Name of Solen Aum Solen - - let it ring - let it ring -- Let the mountains bow low in humbleness before the Name - - let the rivers rush to listen --

Let the birds hush their singing - to listen -- Let the fires blaze forth that all be delighted -- Let the waters wash clean the beds of the passionate - let the harlot be cleansed - and bring forth the pure in heart Let the hare cease his running - and listen -- Let the pages of time be purged of their errors - - let the Hand of God write thereupon in Light, Truth - which hast been hidden - covered up by the blindness of him which hast thot himself wise - - MAN is his name - I say: "MAN is his name"--

In <u>his</u> conceit he hast thot himself wise - - now he shall stand as one in the balance - he shall see himself as one on whose shoulders rests the responsibility of cleaning his own house - of cleaning himself -- And for this is it said: Arise from thine lethargy - and prepare to receive Me and of Me - - so be it I shall wait - I shall wait for their preparation.

I am in the mood to give unto them as they are prepared to receive So be it the law - when they are prepared to receive Me - I shall come in and sup with them - and we shall have the sweet Communion - which shall fill their hearts with such joy - such as they have not known --

So be it - I bring the Sweet Sonnet of Spring -- I bring the Sweet Sonnet of Noon - - and there is no strain of sorrow within it - for it is of the Spirit that I speak - and the Spirit quickeneth - and makes glad the heart - which shall know no fear -- Peace I bestow upon thee Mine Beloved --

I say: Peace - Peace - Peace be upon thee - and let not Peace escape thee - for the Peace I bring is Eternal - - not of a moment - not of a day but Eternal --

Let thine hand be Mine - let thine Voice be Mine - and speak forth that which I put into thy mouth - and ye shall abide in the House of the Lord in Perfect Peace --

Such is Mine Word at this hour -- Peace - Peace - Perfect Peace - Mine Beloved --

= Recognition - Gratitude =

So the time comes that we gather by the River - where flows the Waters of Life Eternal - where flows the Life which is endowed unto All men, All mankind -- We shall partake of this Water which flows from the Heart of God Our Father --

The flow is of Him - from Him - and therein we have our being - therein we have our communion - therein we bathe - therein we are cleansed - therein we are purified --

The purification is of Him - - for this hast He bid us come - and be cleansed -- For this hast He said: "Come unto Me - and be cleansed" - for from out the Heart of God flows the purifying Waters - which cleans and heals --

No sorrow too deep - no night so black - no storm too great - that the purifying Waters cannot overcome - for it is by His Grace that we are provided such power - the cleansing - purifying power - without stint - without price --

We pay homage unto Our Source - we accept that which He - Our Father hast provided --

We give thanks for such provision - such Grace - and Mercy - - for such protection and Love - - for the day at hand - and for the Abundance of Light now coming forth from the Eternal Haven of Beauty - Love Supreme - and from the Eternal Throne of Our Father --

He is co-existent with the All Wise Council - - with the Great and Mighty Council - - with the Host of Hosts --

He is the King - of Kings - - He is the One - and Only King of Glory, He reigneth Supreme -- He resteth not His foot on any thing which was - or which is --

He resteth Not His Hand on One thing - He is the ONE over ALL - IN ALL - and for that He is sufficient unto Himself - - He needs no resting place - He is That - He is the Beginning - the End - the First and the Last - HE IS ALL - within and without - for out from Him All Eternalities cometh - All things exist -- All things move and have their being in Him - for He is the Cause of Being - Worlds without end --

Beside Him there is none other - worthy of the Name Solen Aum Solen --

Beside Him there is none other which is Solen Aum Solen -- So be it He is the One and Only Source of <u>thy</u> being - of Mine Being - - therefore let us Praise His Name forever and forever --

Amen and Amen --

Amen So be it --

= The Greatest Project =

So be it that I am come at this hour - as the one prepared to give unto thee this word -- It behooves Me to say that I am He which is responsible for this part of the Great Plan - as is given unto Me by the Mighty Council -- I am the Head Councilor - yet - I am not alone in this the Greatest Project yet undertaken --

I say - We place before the Council the Plan - and We will - if you please - vote upon each and every mandate-- We are as One Man - of One Mind in this - "<u>The</u> <u>Freedom</u> <u>of Man</u>" --

We sit in Council that each and every one might Know his part - and be as ones in Authority - - and that each be prepared for his part - each be informed of all aspects of the Plan - - and there is no misunderstanding - about any point in question --

We are of like mind - and we are not of a mind to belittle any member of the Council - or anyone with whom we are associated --

We are aware of all points of the law - and the assignments are in no wise made lightly - or without great thot-- Each assignment is carefully assessed - and considered - then - the matter is placed before the Council - and when it is found to be befitting - we call forth the One on whose shoulders it falls to do a certain part -- We give unto him ample time for preparation - - and - the grooming completed - he then goes forth as one prepared - - he then is as one prepared thru long training - and thru Great trials and testing -- When he hast gained in Knowledge - and Wisdom - he is given a Greater part - then upon him falls Greater responsibility --

Greater Wisdom is his - and Greater Strength he hast gained - thru his rigorous training - as a Neophyte - as a Steward - and when he is sufficiently prepared - he goes forth as one prepared to bring about the deliverance of a flock - which is given unto him - which is assigned unto him -- He is responsible for his flock - - he is as the Shepherd of that flock which is entrusted into his keeping -So be it - he hast proven himself trustworth - and he hast proven his worth as a Shepherd - he hast found that his joy comes from Service rendered -- So be it that he shall find his reward to be Great - in the harvest which shall be to his credit --

= The Shepherd's Blessings =

Let it be understood that I - as the Shepherd of the Great Flock - stand with raised hand - that All the Shepherds which I now send forth be as the fold which is kept for them - as the flock which have been gathered in - that they be prepared for the harvest which is <u>now</u> ripe - and the reaping begun - - so be it that I am prepared to bring them back even as I send them out -- So be it and Selah --

= The Court =
Trial / Testimony

Sori Sori -- Mine Beloved:

This is the hour that I shall speak unto thee - and ye shall record it for them which are prepared to receive it -- They shall have it as I give it unto thee -- Put not thine own interpretation upon it - for they shall put theirs upon it - for it shall mean unto each - that which he is prepared to see - to hear --

There shall be ones which will find herein the answer unto their prayers - - others shall find condemnation - - others shall find justification for their foolishness - - others - for their belief in righteousness for righteousness' sake - - others - shall find herein justification for their disbelief --

Now unto them which read - I say: Read with eyes that See - ears that hear - a heart that understands the things of Spirit - for that which I say - concerns the Spirit - is of SPIRIT --

I say: Read with the Spirit of understanding - that ye fall not into the pit - for it is said: "Woe unto them which spit upon the WORD"--

I say - I have prepared for thee a portion which ye have received - and others which awaits thee - - and as ye are prepared so shall ye receive --

Ye shall open thine eyes - and ye shall see that which is written in the parts which ye have received - and ye shall then be prepared for that which is to follow --

Ye shall be as ones placed upon the witness stand - ye shall either bear witness of ME - or ye shall perjure thy Self --

Now it is said: "Betray not thine own Self" For it is now come when thine testimony shall be asked of thee - and ye shall either affirm or deny that which hast been said --

Ye shall either testify for Me or against Me - for there shall be "The Trial" - the testing shall come!

Ye shall choose either way - yet it is said: <u>Ye shall stand firm</u>! Ye shall know that which ye do - for in the time of testing ye shall not forget that which I have said! Ye shall find it shall profit thee to remember - and ye shall fear not - for I am with thee unto the end --

Feign not wisdom! yet - ye shall be assured that I am with thee! I shall not forsake thee in the time of trial -- Justice is Mine - and I am not of a mind to give Mine sheep into the wolves!

Pray ye that ye let not thine tongue betray thee -- Pray ye - that thy foot slips not -- Pray ye - that thine hand slips not -- Pray ye - that the enemy overcome thee not --

For I say unto thee: He - the enemy - would be unto thee great power in the time of fear - and weakness -- I am thy Shield and thy Buckler - I am thy Rod and thy Staff - I am thy Strength in the time of weakness I bid thee - I entreat thee - lean on Me - give unto Me thine hand - and KNOW ye - that I Am with thee - - yet - ye shall choose which way ye go --

I offer Mine hand - Mine assistance - yet I do not impose upon thy will -- Therefore I say unto thee: "Choose ye which way" --

Too - I say: "Follow ye Me - and I shall deliver thee out of bondage".

I deliver thee not into the hands of the enemy - I deliver thee not into the hands of the accuser - the jailer - I deliver thee not unto the lion's den --

I say: I am He - which is Sent that ye perish not -- I Am He - which is come that ye be delivered out of bondage -- So be it and Selah --

Rest with assurance that I Am come to find Mine own -- Yet - I call unto All that they might choose - that they might Know Mine Voice - - and unto them which hear - I say: Come - Come - Come - follow ye Me Unto them which come - I say unto them: "Peace - Peace - Peace - blessed be thou - for thou hast Come" --

And these shall I shield - for I am their Shield and their Buckler - I am their Provider - I am their Stay for in Me "Mine Flock" is staid - - and no wolves - neither the enemy enters in - for I say: I Am the Door Keeper - and it is well guarded - none pilfer the latch - none put their foot upon the hearth stone of Mine abode unprepared - for I am the Host within Mine House - and I say: NONE defile Mine House - NONE I say -- Therein are no traitors - no enemies - for I have said: "None enter in unprepared - none deceive Me" - I Know them - I see them as friend or foe!

I Know them for that which they are - they deceive Me not!!

I say unto ALL: "Come - Come - Come"- and they choose which way they shall go -- I make no promises - I abide by the law - I play no favorites - I am an impartial One -- I say: Obey ye the Mandates: - obey ye the law - and ye have heard it said: "Prepare ye for the Greater Part" hast it not been said: "As ye prepare thyself - so shall ye receive"? It is

So! Therefore I repeat: "AS YE ARE PREPARED SO SHALL YE RECEIVE!"--

Let thine testimony be yea - or nay - it matters not - - ye shall abide by thine own / and by thine own desire to serve - either the Light or the dark -- For the dark one stands ready to go to battle - he is armed with the tongue of the intellect - the weapon of the learned - in the way of speech -- He hast the will to give unto thee the comforts - of life - <u>for a time</u> - as his trap --

He promises "Comfort" - he gives unto thee words flattering unto thine ears - - and chains for thy hands and feet -- He even gives unto thee power to forge thine own legirons -- He gives thee the rope for thine own neck - that ye hang thine self - - then he <u>washes</u> <u>his</u> <u>hands</u> - and declares himself innocent of any "Sins" - for he has allowed thee to follow him - and thou hast put thine own head into <u>his</u> noose -- Wherein canst he be blamed for any wrong doing? Why hast thou been so foolish? Hast thou not been warned of his trickery? "TRICKERY" I say! Be ye aware of him which promises thee luxury - and a seat in high places --

I say - ye earn thy own way - ye <u>earn</u> thy own honors - thine own salvation - and ye have been told: "As ye earn so do ye learn - as ye learn so do ye earn" -- And it is for thine own good that I say: "Be ye aware of him who says: 'Come I shall give unto thee ease - power - prestige and grandeur of palace - things of the world'- for I say these are traps - these are the trapping of the enemy"--

Behold ye the things Eternal - the things which perish not - for the things of Spirit I would give unto thee - as thine Eternal Inheritance -- The things of Earth shall pass away and be no more - yet I say: Ye shall inherit Eternal Life -- Be ye as one prepared to enter in - into the place wherein there is no want - no sorrow - no pain - no darkness - - for this is Mine Word unto thee this day: "Choose ye which way ye shall go"--

Thou hast been given FREE WILL - I say: Use it to thine own everlasting profit -- So be it I am thine Elder Brother - which hast gone before thee - that ye might find thine way -- It is given unto Me to be the Wayshower - - I have said: I KNOW the Way - for I have gone before thee to prepare the Way --

I am no stranger to man - - man is not strange unto Me - for I have walked the Earth as man - man of flesh - - I Know the trials and temptations - the pain and sorrows of flesh --

I too - Know - the joy of attainment - the joy of Victory won --

I know the battle grounds - I Know the place of Peace - I Know where Peace abides - - and peace and war are not compatible - they are not g__oo__d frien__ds__ - they are opposites - one of the Light - one of the dark.

I ask of thee: Where dost thou make a mockery of Mine sayings - Mine Words? Art thou prepared to stand with Me - and answer these questions of thine own Self? What shall thine answer be - shall ye think to deceive ME?

I say: I am __not__ deceived by thine WORDS - neither by thine ACTS I see thine heart - thine light - - by thine light I say!! Keep thine hand to the plow - make clean thy furrow - and let no plow be found rusting.

Place thine hand to the plow - I say! Plow clean thy furrow - make strait the furrow - for it cometh quickly - that ye shall see the preparation ye have made --

I say - the fields are now being prepared - the fields are <u>Now being prepared</u>!!

I have called for Mine plowmen - and I have instructed them - - I have given unto them the particulars - I have given unto them the instructions necessary unto the work at hand --

I have placed within their hand the plow shares - and said: "Go ye out and prepare the fields for the coming day"-"for the season changeth the season changeth - the Season Changeth I say!" - - and ye have been called to the field which shall be cultivated - and then cometh the time of sowing - then the time of harvest -- I ask of thee: What shall thy harvest be? - Wheat or tares? - Thistles - thorns - or garlands of posies garlands for thy forehead - garlands of thistles - or posies soft upon thy brow?

I ask of thee: What soweth thou? Hast thou tilled thine field? Hast thou cultivated the thorn - or the posy?

Be ye as one prepared to receive thine garland - which thou hast made with thine own hands -- So be it thine - - wear it with grace - or - disgrace - as thou will --

I say: Peace - Peace - Peace unto all men - - yet - hast thou chosen the Way of Peace - or hast thou chosen the way of destruction?

These questions I would have thee consider well - and be not so foolish as to THINK I ask of thee <u>foolish</u> Questions!

I AM HE which Knows thee better than ye knowest thyself - man - O Man - I speak out this day that ye might know thyself -- I say: Be ye up and about the FATHER'S BUSINESS!

Behold ye the Light Which I Am - behold ye the Way Which I Am and ye shall find it shall profit thee --

I am Sent of Him Which is the source of thy Being - and unto Him all the Praise - and the Glory -- Let thine hands be His - thine feet be His -- Let thine Voice be His - let thine tongue praise His Name - - let thine feet be swift to do His bidding - thine hands swift to do His Work Let thine heart be His Heart - let it beat out the rhythm of life - His Life which He hast endowed unto thee - for it is His to give - HIS to take - be it ever So -- So let it be - Amen and Selah --

= Light - Substance =

Sori Sori -- Beloved: -

This is My time with thee - and it is given unto Me to say: that ye shall be the one chosen for this part -- There hast been others called - but thou art chosen --

Be ye as one prepared - for this are ye the one chosen -- Present this part unto them which have prepared themself to receive it --

Ye may do with it as ye will - yet I say - it is well to present it unto them which are seeking the Light -- While all that say: "We seek the Light" are not of a mind to receive - for they know not that which they say - they know not the meaning of "THE LIGHT"- for they have not found it -- They have sought the pleasures of flesh - and called it "lite", lightly they speak of the very Substance of their Being!

They are as children - inasmuch as they know not the meaning of their words - spoken so lightly -- When they come to know what Light is - they need go no place to seek or find - for they are within it - it is their Sustaining Power - and their Being depends upon it - for It they have their Being -- They are prone to look in dark places - and for "things" as props - and stepping stones -- I say they use these props as crutches - they ask another's support - knowing not that they have their being within the Very Substance of Life / Light - - It is the Reality of Being --

Out of this Substance is the things born -- Out of this Substance is it held within form -- Out of this Substance cometh the seen -- The material substance seen is but the unseen - made seen -- It is lowered in its frequency - into the denser - lower frequency - where ye may see touch - feel or hear - as it may be --

These things I would have ye add unto the other part of this "Book" which ye are now preparing - which shall follow that first one -- The second one shall be given in parts as ye wish - and it shall be as ye will the parts may be large or small - and they shall be as the parts of a Whole - which shall be designated as book two of the Host -- While it is said it shall simply be "The Door"- is it not? Now it is given unto Me to see them pass thru "The Door" and enter in - - this shall be cause for rejoicing--

= Dedications of Book Two =

Now this Second Book of which this is but one small part - shall be called: "The Book of The Hosts" "The Door" - - Dedicated unto All who enter in -- They shall be blest -- So be it and Selah --

This shall be Mine Word unto them - and I shall be amongst The Host to receive them -- So be it and Selah --

I am with thee this day - - So be it I bless thee with Mine Presence and Mine Being -- Amen and Selah -

Recorded by Sister Thedra

= The Talkers =
Thinkers

Sori Sori -- Be ye as Mine Voice unto them which are of a mind to learn Say unto them in Mine name - that I am now prepared to bring them out of darkness -- I am come that they be brot out - - yet they shall prepare themself to receive Me - and of Me --

There is but little time - for the time is now come when they shall face their own foolishness - or they shall find their freedom - - I say - "their freedom" for they have not known freedom - neither have they been free - - they speak of freedom - yet they know it not --

They have not been free ever - for they were born under the yoke - they have been as wanderers on the periphery -- They have not seen the Inner Temple - for they are on the outer side of the periphery - and they see not that which is within the Inner Temple --

They know not that they are in bondage - they <u>think</u> themself wise knowing not from whence they came - neither whither they goest --

Now it is come when they shall awaken unto their sad state -- They are in bondage - they are in darkness - ignorant of that which awaits them - when they are prepared to receive it --

= **The Host** =

The time is come when <u>many</u> shall go forth - prepared to give unto them that which shall profit them - - yet it is said: "Some shall reject them and that which they bring"--

It is said - that "It shall be as the personal touch" - for each unto his own - - each shall go unto his next of kin - and he shall touch him - he shall speak softly - words familiar unto them - and they shall understand that which is said - and he shall bless them -- He shall be unto them that which The Father would have him be - and he shall be as one prepared to awaken them - - he shall be as one Sent - and therein is wisdom - for there are many which know Me not - many which deny Me - - yet they shall know their own --

And they shall have proof! They shall be as ones aware - and they shall ask of the one Sent for his help - and it shall be the beginning of his preparation - and he shall be led gently - and therein is wisdom --

I say: Gently he shall be led - and no place shall they be betrayed - There are many which shall fall down and worship him which is Sent, yet he shall find his way - and he shall profit thereby - for he shall learn wherein he is staid -- So be it and Selah --

Now he which is Sent unto thee shall come bearing gifts - and he shall be as one familiar unto thee - and ye shall accept him in Mine name - for I have Sent him -- So be it and Selah --

Beloved: I speak unto thee as once I did long ago - when I held you as a child -- Again I hold them as a child - for I see thee as one humble as a little child - You come asking nought for thyself - a precious child Behold ye the Great Shining One - Whose shoes I am not worthy to tie

I say - ye are beyond me - yet I see thee as one shining and sweet as a babe in arms -- Well do I remember thee as a babe - my first born -- Now I await thy coming - for Great art thou - Great I say -- I await thy coming - for there is Great things in store for us - Great Work allotted us - and when ye arrive into this place - we shall go forth into Greater fields - for the harvest is heavy - and we shall be as ones prepared to go forth that we bring in the harvest --

While I am about it - let me say that I have seen thy effort on the Cover - and it is well done my dear -- Fear not for the opinions of others I say it is well done - and it is befitting that ye have made such progress and it shall be as acceptable unto us --Who is there to judge thee - and thy efforts? I say: Fear not for it is acceptable -- Remember - I said we work with "Ideas" - there is the Idea -- Let them learn from the "Idea"- for it shall profit them -- So many want it spelled out for them - yet they shall learn to spell for themself --

When it is written - they must first learn to read - - when it is spoken they first must learn to hear --

This is not idle speech - you know what I say -- So be it we shall learn to communicate without words - - this is most practical - - let us begin --

Pay ye no heed to the simple prattle of the unlearned - the unwise who think themself wise - for they are not of a mind to bestir themself Make no pretense of preachments for them - they shall find their way So be it and Selah -- Good night my Beloved -

= Obedience =

Sori Sori -- For this time let us speak of obedience - of loyalty --

This is for the most part the greatest of the training of the neophyte for he has to first learn obedience unto the law -- He has to learn from whence his blessing cometh -- He gives himself in honest preparation and service - asking no reward - no glory - no honors - for his honor cometh from his honest service rendered selflessly - without thot of self.

For when a man works for self - he is as one on whose head rests the crown of thorns - - he hast placed his hand upon the scales - that they balance in his favor -- He hast been in no wise aware of his fellow's welfare -- He thinks to deceive his fellows - and gain favor in the sight of his neighbor -- For this hast he betrayed himself and his trust - he has betrayed himself - hast he not? Let us say he hast short-changed himself - for it is so --

Now it is said - he shall walk upright - and obey the law - - he shall do unto others as he would they do unto him -- He shall walk as he would have them - for he shall find that they are but the image of himself - - they shall too betray themself - and he shall be as the recipient of that which he hast sent forth - for it shall boomerang upon him - and he shall find that he hast profited nought by his deceit -- So be it that he shall learn the way of the neophyte - then when he hast proven himself worthy - he shall be given Greater things to do - greater parts - Greater Responsibility--

= Cause & Effect =

This is but the beginning - for it is seen that they have not as yet comprehended the fullness of the Plan -- They have not been as the one with the Greater Vision -- They have not been as one which stands on the Summit - and sees with the Greater Vision -- They see that which they see - as but partly - in part -- They know not that which they see is but the manifestation of that which they see not --

Now it is said: "Seek ye the Light and it shall not be hidden" - knowest thou the meaning of this? I say: Seek ye that which is back of the manifestation - the Cause of the manifestation - that which is the CAUSE of ALL manifestation - the FIRST CAUSE -- "Seek ye first the Kingdom of God" - Knowest the meaning of this?

Wherein is the Kingdom of God? I say it is not of man - man's world the material world - not of Earth! It is of the World which ye shall come to know -- Then ye shall Know as I Know - then - there shall be no mysteries - no ties - no boundaries - no impenetrable walls or barriers for ye shall be one with the Law - One with thy Cause of Being - and ye shall stand shorn of all thy preconceived opinions - and ideas of the "Father's Kingdom" which shall come on Earth - as thou hast prayed.

Yet it shall not be a Kingdom such as thou hast imaged - I say: "Man - O Man - thou hast imaged vain imaginings"-- Vain indeed - for thou hast been as ones putting thine own words into Mine mouth - - thou hast written them and given unto Me credit for speech which I have not uttered - for I am not of a mind to speak that which is not of TRUTH - not of the LIGHT - for I say: I am responsible for Mine Words - and I have never given unto thee that which I now deny --

For I say unto thee: I am accountable unto the One which hast Sent Me forth - I am accountable unto the Law - even as thou art - - yet I come under the Greater Law - under the Divine Law - which is yet above that of nature -- Yet it is not without its part - but the laws of "Nature" are natural laws which govern the seen world - as it is seen -

yet it is unseen. The law only brings into the seen - that which is not seen - while the Unseen is ever greater - and more potent than the seen.

Therefore it is said: "Seek ye the Kingdom of God" - that which is back - of the manifestation --

That which is back/ the Cause of - the "Natural" manifestation is of the Father the Cause -- It is said: "See the Hand of God move" - I say - it moveth! See it - behold - it moveth - it causeth the axis to spin - thy Earth to rotate thereon - therein - within its orbit -- It brings the seasons, the Sun to rise - to set in the appointed time - - It causes the unseen to be made seen -- Therefore I say: "Seek ye the Kingdom of God" - for hast He not created the Heaven - and the Earth? Wherefore cometh thy knowledge? I ask of thee wherefore cometh thy knowledge?

Thinkest thou O Man - that thou seest that which causeth thy being which hast held thee fast in the hours of thy unknowing?

I ask thee - whence goest thou? Whither come thou? It is not a small foolish question I ask of thee! I ask thee to ponder well that which I have put before thee -- See that which is written in the "Book of Life"- open up thine eyes - behold the things placed before thee - - See the Works of God - for His finger hast power - His finger - hast power to move the planets - for He is the Creator - He is the Planner - the Architect - the Husbandman --

He hast the Power - the Authority - for He is Eternally the Father of His Creation -- He Creates Well/ Good - according unto the LAW which is Eternal - therefore He is the Law - and He is the First and the Last - Alpha & Omega -- He hast the First and the Last Word - He sends out - He brings back that which He sends out - and it follows as the night the day - ye shall return unto the place of thy beginning -- So be it and Selah --

Yet - I say: This is the hour of thy calling - this is the Day -- I say: Ye shall heed the Call - and answer - - come forth in this day - or - ye shall wait long - and thy waiting shall be long indeed - - sad indeed shall it be –

For the WORD hast gone out: "COME HOME - COME HOME"- and ye shall come of thine own accord - or ye shall wait! - It is of the Greatest concern unto The Mighty Host - that ye hear - yet - none shall impose upon thy free will - for it is <u>thine</u> - thy own precious gift - - do with it as ye will --

Yet it is said: Fashion for thyself no legirons - for We - "The Host" come that ye be free -- Come - as thou will - stay - as thou will - - for it is for thy sake that We come -- We of The Host have won our freedom thru obedience and dedication unto the Will of God Our Father -- So be it that We speak of things profitable unto thee -- So be it We stand by to assist thee in the hour of need - ye but have to accept us for that which We are - and obey the law --

We have won our freedom - even as ye shall win thine - by adherence unto the law -- Fear not that ye be misled when ye obey the mandates laid before thee --

It is the law of the One - the law of the Eternal - Shining One of which I speak -- Ye shall remember thy blessings - count them one by one - then two by two's - then by the dozens - for they shall be multiplied a thousand fold! So be it and Selah --

= Keep Active Thy Humility =

Sori Sori -- Be ye responsible for this Mine Word which I give unto thee this day -- Ye shall place it within the book which is now being prepared - and it shall go in parts - or in one whole - as ye will - - yet the end is not near -- So be it that I say unto them which shall receive it - they have not as yet conceived the IDEA of the Whole Plan - for it is as yet not revealed in its entirety --

They shall be prepared for such revelation - and therefore I say: Follow where I lead thee -- I shall lead thee gently and surely - - I shall be thy Shield and thy Buckler - and ye shall not want - neither shall ye fall --

= Learning without Understanding is Dangerous =

Be as one prepared - and ye shall be led <u>gently</u> - I say "gently" - for there shall be no shock - no place wherein ye might trip and fall -- I say I am the "Way Shower" and I know that which I am about - - I give unto thee no more than ye can bear -- So be it that I am mindful of thine capacity - - it is said thine capacity shall be increased -- So be it and Selah --

Now it shall be remembered that ye are but beginning thine climb - thy ascent -- Ye shall not find a resting place for there is Greater heights before thee -- Think ye not that ye have attained unto Great W<u>isdo</u>m - for I say unto thee - thy learning shall profit thee little - should ye sit upon the way - and fret for the ones yet below --

I say: "Come <u>YE</u> forth - and I shall give unto THEE as ye are <u>pre</u>pared to receive"--

= Warning to the Zealots =

Ye shall be as one blest to come -- It is said - ye shall not fret for the ones which sit by the wayside - and cry for thy assistance -- While they too - are commanded to "Come" - they drag their feet - and ask of thee thy time and strength -- So be it that ye shall be unto them the messenger - - deliver into their hands the Word - then turn them loose and let them do as they will with it -- <u>Feign</u> <u>not</u> <u>Wisdom</u> - for thou <u>art</u> <u>not</u> <u>as</u> <u>yet</u> <u>on</u> <u>the</u> <u>Summit</u> --

Thou hast as yet not attained the Greater heights - thou art yet not on the Higher Ground -- Be ye as one prepared - for the next part - which shall be revealed unto thee - - for it is said: Greater revelation shall be given unto them - as they are prepared to receive -- So be it and Selah --

Be ye aware of Mine Words - treat them not lightly! - For I say - ye shall be as one responsible for that which ye do with them -- So be it and Selah --

Say unto them as I would - that they shall be as ones prepared to receive - and they shall first seek Truth - and it shall be given unto them to know the true from the false-- So be it and Selah --

Now - <u>ye</u> shall be as one held responsible for that which ye do with these Mine Words -- Ye shall hold them unto <u>thyself</u> - until thou hast made them thine own - and when thou hast found the meaning therein THEN ye shall pass them on unto thy brethren - for it behooves Me to say - that as <u>he</u> is prepared so shall he - receive -- Unto the ones of little sight - unto <u>him</u> little is seen - - unto the blind nothing is seen -- So be it that I say: "OPEN UP THINE EYES that <u>YE</u> might SEE" --

So be it that I shall teach thee of things Greater than which ye have dreamed -- Ye shall find that Mine House is not empty -- <u>Mine</u> store is rich indeed! - and there are no sleepers within Mine House --

= Nothing Hidden =

Rest ye securely within the Knowledge that I am aware of thine own waywardness - thy fickleness - thine wonton - thine rebellion -- Yet - I say: When ye have seen that which I <u>HAVE</u> said - ye shall be as one prepared to go forward as a mighty soldier - prepared to do battle against the foe --

= The Initiate =

Then ye shall step forth in Great strength - prepared to go forward as one of the Mighty Host - as one of The Host -- So be it I have spoken - hast thou heard Me? Hast thou comprehended that which I have said? Let thine eyes be opened - thine ears be made to hear - - let thine way be Mine Way - and I shall touch thee -- So be it and Selah --

= Thot Forms - Symbols =

Sori Sori-- Beloved: It is again time for this our communication -- I say "Our communication" for are we not in communication? Are there not many questions in thy mind? and do I not see them?

Now let it be said: - that I see thy questions - unwritten tho they be neither are they spoken -- It is as tho you had a symbol for each and every thot - and these thots transcribed into color symbols - - each one I can read as you would read the signs on a calendar -- While the signs are not the days - they represent the day - accurate for thy own use - or for thy own purpose --

Now - for My purpose or use - I use your thot pattern or symbols - they serve My purpose - and My purpose is to help with the awakening of mankind - for I come as one of the Host -- I come as one prepared to See - and to assist in the awakening -- I see the thots - and as they are unaware of their thot patterns - they draw many unto them which would be unto them their undoing - should they not have our assistance --

I say We guard them which have no knowledge of Us - The Host - While they are not what we call evil - neither are they of a mind to accept Us their Benefactors - for they know not that We are their Benefactors - - they have not been enlightened on this subject of communication -- They have feared the "DEAD"! O - could they Know the love We bear them! Could they see with eyes of Spirit - they would cry for joy! Never in fear - No - never in fear - - so gladly would they come unto us - and be glad for our assistance --

Let us commune one with the other - and love them who understand not -- Love them which persecute thee - and they shall learn that which they have ridiculed - is but the Way of the Lord - which shall be as the way of the learned - - in this I mean: This shall become common knowledge unto them - ere they enter into the Holy of Holies -- So be it and Selah --

Put thy pen unto the paper - and record that which I say unto thee - and it shall profit thee to record that which is said - and they shall be blest to receive it -- So be it and Selah --

Mine Word shall be as thine - and ye shall speak the words I put into thy mouth - and none shall deny them - for it is as tho I am speaking out of My own mouth -- I shall loose thy tongue - and ye shall speak freely and knowingly - for I have decreed it - and I am come that ye be blest -- So be it I am He which hast lain Mine hand upon thy head in Holy benediction - and pronounced thee Mine Priestess -- Now I have said unto thee: "Ye shall have another Gift" - and it is so -- And so be it and Selah -- I pronounce thee Mine Voice/ Mine Hand Maiden - in whom I am well pleased -- So be it I am Sananda - and I am He which is Sent of Mine Father that His Will be done in Me - thru Me - and by Me -- So let it be - Amen and Selah--

= The Flight =

Sori Sori -- Be ye as one prepared to receive Him which is sent as one of the Host - for he comes in the Name of the Father and the Son -- It is now come when He shall speak as One sent - and He speaks with the Authority and power of One Sent -- So be it ye shall be blest to receive Him -- Amen and Selah --

Beloved: It is with great joy that I am come -- It is given unto Me to be One of the Host - and I speak with the Authority which is invested within Me by and thru the Mighty Council -- They have put within My hand the power to speak unto thee by this means - - let it profit all who read -- So be it I see this Work go forward as a great Vine which has its roots in fertile soil -- So be it and Selah --

Now ye shall give this Mine part unto them - with the last part - and it shall be like unto the others - inasmuch as it shall not be changed or edited - for it shall serve its purpose well -- Forget not that this is given for a purpose -- Fret not over the ones which shall turn their back upon thee for they shall find that it hast profited them nought - - they shall find they have tript themself up - tript over their own feet - - and they shall remember their own clumsiness - and be as ones reminded of their own puny way - and see the foolishness of their own opinions and preconceived ideas -- So be it I ask nought of thee - only obedience unto the law - unto which We adhere -- So be it - it is given unto Us to obey - therefore I speak according to the law - the law of Love Eternal for it is by the law that ye shall find the fulfilling - the fulfillment of the law is Love - and Love is the fulfilling of the law - therefore I am allowed to come and speak unto thee that All be blest - even as I --

Bear ye in mind that I come as One of the Host - as One Sent - and I bear thee Good Tidings -- So be it ye shall have upon thy head the Laurel Wreath - and it shall weigh lightly upon thy brow - for ye shall not be bowed down by it - neither shall ye be as one on whose head rests the thistle crown which shall prick the flesh -- And remember this: I am come by the Grace of the Father - and by the consent of The Great and Mighty Council - therefore I am qualified to speak thusly --

Be ye as one on whose head I place M<u>ine</u> hand in Holy benediction and I pronounce the WORD - and it shall as Mine testimony unto thee and ye shall be as a living witness of the WORD - as a living testimony of The WORD - and ye shall walk amongst them Knowingly - and without fear -- And ye shall be aware of them which cry out for help - and them which are weary - and them which have a will to turn from their puny way - and serve the Light - and them which are prepared to be brot out of darkness --

I say: You shall walk with them - and counsel them as ye have been counseled - and ye shall go into the places wherein they are - and touch them - and they shall Know they have been touched -- So be it and Selah --

This I would say unto thee: Bear ye in mind that many are come unto thee this day that they bear witness of the LAW - the Light - and they have been unto themself true - and they shall not betray their trust So be it that I am come as one of them -- I put forth Mine hand even as they - in Holy benediction - that they too - might receive from Me Mine blessing -- So be it that I am He which cometh as an unknown - for I say unto thee: Thou Knowest Me not by name - yet ye shall come to know Me - for I have walked by thy side as a Brother - that ye be protected from the darkness of men - from the pit falls --

I have seen thy frailties and weakness - and I have given of Mine Strength in the time of sore trial - and I have given of Mine Love when they have turned unto thee their backs - and when they have asked of thee more than their share -- So be it I know thine part - and I come that it be done in honor and dignity - and no man shall stay thine progress - neither thy flight - for thy flight shall be as the speed of thot - and no man shall follow thee in thy flight -- No man shall know whither thou goest - - whither thou goest - I shall go - for I am thy Elder Brother - Sent to shield and protect thee in thy of flight - So be it and Selah --

Be ye as one prepared for the Greater Part -- For this do I speak unto thee - Amen - Amen and Selah --

Recorded by Sister Thedra

For the Record

Sori Sori -- Let it be recorded that which I say unto thee - and let it go down in history that All might Know that which I say unto thee - - it is for the Good of All that I speak thusly --

Many yet unborn shall bear witness of Mine Words - which I give unto thee - for they are recorded on the pages of time - wherein they may be found by All which are prepared to read --

There is but the ones which have been unto themself true – which shall enter into the secret place of the Most High Living God - for I say: Therein shall be no traitors/ none unprepared --

= The Traitors =

So be it that I have given unto them the Golden Key - and they have mocked Me - - they have turned from Me as if I were an imposter --

I say unto them - they are as ones under the black cape - they are as ones on whose shoulders rests Great responsibility - for they shall be responsible for their own salvation -- They shall be as ones responsible for that which they do with the Word which I give unto them --

They shall be allowed to dwell within their own environment - and they shall come to weary of that which they have created -- So be it and Selah -- They shall find that they have made for themself their own path and it shall be as one of thorns - which shall tear the flesh - - and they shall lament their lot --

So be it that they have betrayed their trust - for have they not been entrusted with The Word? And have they been unto Me a friend? Have they not sought out their soothsayers and necromancers? the magician and the false gods - who promise them great miracles - and signs? Wherein have they been Mine friends? Have I not given unto them that which should bless them - and that which should profit them?

Yet - have they followed Me - have they heeded unto Mine COUNSEL? Have they given unto Me their heart - their hand - themself in wholly Surrender? Wherein do they deceive themself? I say - they do deceive themself --

= The Waiting =

Have I not given unto them the Key? The Key I have placed within their hand - yet they know not wherein it is - for they have not seen that which is obvious - - they look and see not - they hear and comprehend not -- So be it they shall wait - wait - wait I say! - For they have put their foot in a hole - - they shall now find that I shall withdraw Mine hand - and they shall do that which they will -- So be it and Selah --

= No Hiding Place =

Pay ye heed - fret not for them which turn their face from thee -- Pity them not for their wait - which shall be long - - yet it shall be a time of ripening - and when they are ripe - then they shall be brot in - and put into their proper place - and it shall be as they are prepared - for each shall be in his proper place -- None shall be lost from Mine sight -- I know them by name - number and color - I see them and know them - each and every one - for there is no hiding place!

= Deliverance =

I am come that they be brot out - - yet it is said - they shall come of their own accord -- So be it the law --

I am come that they be prepared to go where I go - that they be prepared to enter into Mine place of abode - wherein there is no sorrow no darkness - no bondage -- So be it I have spoken - I am speaking - and I shall speak again and again - for I am NOT finished!

= The Blessing =

I am come unto thee that they be blest - and they shall remember thee as they remember Me - for art thou not Mine hand and Mine Voice unto them -- So be it and Selah -- I am He which is Sent that ye be blest forever and forever -- Amen - So be it --

= What is the Host? =

Sori Sori -- Now I speak out as One man - for I am the Host of the Host I speak for the "Host" - as the Host - for I am the Host -- while the body of the Host is made up of many - many - many I say! They are of One Mind - one plan - one mind to serve the Great and Divine Plan -- They serve in numbers as one man - for they are not divided by opinions and preconceived ideas --

= The Concern of the Host =

They are not concerned with the puny concerns of man -- They are only concerned with Man's Freedom from bondage - from his ignorance - and from the traps in which he hast so unwittingly put his foot --

The Host is as the Benefactors of man - - they are of one body - one mind - one concern - and they know the part that each hast been given. Yet all parts fit into the Whole of the Plan - they go forth as a Mighty Army - to do battle against the foe -- They are well prepared - for they have applied themself aforehand - they have trained diligently for their part --

Now it is said that: "Ye shall be as one of the Host" - it is so - for hast thou not proven thyself - hast thou not trained for thy part?

I say: Thou hast proven thyself - and ye shall now go forth as One with the Host - ye shall go forth as One with Me - and ye shall remember that which I have said - for ye shall go into places new and strange unto thee -- And ye shall have no need of forethot - neither shall ye be as one burdened by the clothing ye shall take - for I say - ye shall be unto thyself sufficient --

Ye shall have no need of bag - or parcel - - ye shall go as if by flight by the swift flight of thot - and none shall deter thee in thy flight - - for the way shall be made strait before thee - and ye shall go and come freely - and ye shall not want -- So be it and Selah -- Ye shall stand as one alert - as one prepared - for the Call cometh - when? - no man knoweth -- He shall wait the Call - and be as one prepared to go where Sent - and come when called - so be it preparedness -- For this have I said: Be ye as one prepared to do that which I give unto thee to do --

Ye have been true unto thy trust - and unto thyself - - so be it it shall profit thee --

Blest is he which walks in the way I point him -- Blest is he which goes where I send him --

Blest is he which awaits Mine direction - for patience is a virtue --

Blest is he which is One with Me - for he shall K<u>no</u>w that which I Know -- So be it and Selah ---

Sori Sori -- Be ye as one on whose head I place Mine hand - and be ye as one blest - for I have declared unto thee the Truth of thine Calling

I have portioned out unto thee thine portion - and I am but begun - - for I say unto thee thine portion is no puny one - not a puny portion - - for it is given unto Me to see that which is kept for thee -- Ye have been as one true unto thyself - - now ye shall be as one blest to go into the place wherein there are records of thine Work - and ye shall review that which ye have accomplished - and ye shall see the fruits of thy labor - So be it it shall profit thee -- It is now come when ye shall be called - and ye shall be as one prepared to enter into the Holy of Holies - and ye shall drink of the Living Water - - - Ye shall partake of Mine Cup - and We shall commune one with the other - and be glad -- So be it and Selah --

I am come that ye might be prepared to go where I go -- So be it that I say unto thee: Come - thou hast heard Me - and responded unto Mine Voice - - thou hast heeded Mine Voice - and now ye shall be as one blest to receive as I have received -- So be it and Selah --

Rememberance Day

Beloved: It is my privilege to speak at this time -- I come with my beloved Teacher - which is also yours - and it gives us of the Host - great joy to have such communion as we are privileged --

For this is the time which has been spoken of - when the heavens should open up - and the Host should come forth - and every eye should see - and every tongue should speak and bear witness of the Glory of Heaven -- They have not interpreted this to be as it is -- they have been as ones looking for great mysterious appearances - and things far beyond reason -- They have been as children in their imaginings and their imagination hast ran riot --

They would not understand the signs and wonders hoped for - should they be given -- Would they not ask further "proof" - for greater signs - more miracles? Who gave credit unto whom - for the miracles already given? Have they accepted these things as true? Have they not denied the "proof" given?

Now they shall ask yet again for greater proof and more miracles - Now let us examine the things which they have called miracles - yet denied and spurned as nought --

= Indecision =

Wherein are they betraying themself? "Wherein do they say they see - and wherein do they say they have not seen?

Now - they have either seen - or they have not seen -- They have given of their own word - that they have seen - - then they say it was as nought? Wherein do they make of themself liars?

Now it is come when they shall stand up and be counted -- They shall bear witness of Me - or they shall deny Me - and that which I have done -- That which I h<u>av</u>e done shall be as a small part of that which I shall do –

= The Wisest One =

That which I shall do shall be as nothing unto that which our beloved Teacher shall do - for He is the Greater - the most powerful - and the Wisest One - Whom We would emulate -- It is for this that I would follow where He leads me - for I know Him to be the Leader of Men - All men would do well to emulate Him --

= Devotion =

I say unto you my Beloved: It is given unto me to see you as one prepared to follow where He leads - and I am glad for your devotion and loyalty - for He is the Great Shining One - on whose countenance I am privileged to look --

I say unto you: It is a privilege indeed to be permitted to behold His Countenance -- Be ye as one - and ye shall be as one forever blest -- So be it and Selah --

You shall know the joy which We know - when you have finished thy mission in flesh - and when you step forth as one free from the bonds of flesh - - for it is given unto thee to feel the pull of atomic substance of Earth - to feel the pull of the gravitation of Earth -- Yet you shall slip the bonds of Earth - and raise as an eagle on wings of light - and the bonds shall be forever broken - - and no more shall ye take upon thyself carnal flesh! No more shall ye walk the way of flesh for it is said: You shall be unto them Sibor - even as He - The Shining One is to you --

No longer shall ye be as one bound by the flesh! No more shall ye walk the roads upon which thy weary feet have trodden - wherein ye have sweated - and suffered thy crucifixion --

Now ye shall go out as one free - free from the fetters of Earth -- Yet Earth shall be unto thee a gem within thy hand - for you shall see her from afar - and yet you shall touch her as a shining jewel to be loved and prized as a thing of beauty - and as a precious gem -- I say - She -

the Earth - shall always hold a spot sacred within thy memory - and you shall be as one which hast past that way - and thy memory of her shall be sweet indeed - for it hast given unto thee footing - and provided for thee in the years of thy training - and it shall serve thee yet - for thou art not finished - thy work not yet completed --

Ye shall be as one long away - and ye shall be as one received into this Mine place - and with Great joy - for I say - it is with Great joy when one returns unto his abiding place --

Now it is Mine part to say: You shall be as one which hast received thine passport - - thine passport is in order - and it behooves me to say I am glad - for I shall await thy coming -- So be it a glad day --

Let it be - for this shall we give eternal thanks unto Him Which hast provided us the strength and the power - that which hast been unto us sufficient unto our coming - for without His help and Wisdom - we would not have been so favored --

I shall praise His Name - and adore Him always -- So be it – Amen.

Like in days of yore - I say unto you my Beloved: "Good night my love" - Some day you shall say unto me: "Good Day"- Dad -

= Who are the Dead? =

Sori Sori -- Be ye as one blest to receive Me this day - and ye shall be blest of the Host of which I am but one - while we are One in body - One in mind - One in purpose -- I am speaking as one - one individual for I am no less the same one which ye have known and still love as "Dad"-- You have learned that I am not "dead" unto you - and for that I am grateful -- Now that ye have had proof of me in thy s<u>lee</u>p - ye know for sure that I am near - I am not far off - - for I am near that you might be better prepared for the part which you are to do - or play -- Now ye shall give unto thyself credit for knowing more than you do --

At times you discount that which you know - - and now you have the assurance that it is I - that it is <u>Not</u> a dream - this communication between us - you and me -- While you do not doubt that the communication between yourself and Our Beloved Teacher is valid - you are oft-times skeptical of mine words - why? I ask why? - Now I see it - - you are wondering at the progress -- Now know ye - that I am not so progressed as thou art --

I am <u>Not</u> so progressed as thou art! This is not of any imagination or flattery - for I am not given to flattery as you know - yet I speak truth and it is shown us here - that you have progressed far beyond me --

Have <u>they</u> not imaged vain imagings? Have they not had their opinions of this side of the "Veil" as well as that one?

It is now come when we see clearly what is meant by: "Entertaining Angels unaware"-- I knew not that I was entertaining one - - that statement is not born of a sense of humor as you think --

I mean - that none of the family knew from whence you came - neither thy mission - for that matter neither did you -- Yet - that matters not -- For that hast it been wise that I go before you - and do the part which has been given unto me to do -- Now do you see - or understand why so many things were done in the years before we were separated? There were so MANY things which we didn't understand - so many fears! so much misunderstanding of that which appeared to be the right way -- The right way was not so clearly seen then - - so many taboos -

so many opinions and misinterpretations of the law - as set before us - by our forerunners --

= The Church =

The church knew no more than we did - - it was a great stumbling block in its ignorance and unknowing - for its interpretation of the <u>law</u> was no more than ours - - the blind leading the blind - - yea - both falleth into the ditch!

Now we have the Greater Vision - the Greater Knowledge - and it is for this that I am permitted to speak -- I come not for a sermon - I simply come that I might be of assistance unto thee - as well as to all who go into this Work with the WILL to learn --

Thy part has not been easy - not at all -- Thy part was given unto thee long ago - even before thou came into flesh - - for I now see the record as it is - as it was - and it is given unto me to see with eyes unveiled - and with clear sight -- I know now what I see - I am the one given the sight to see - - and you now see as thru my eyes - - that is - that which I show you as in visions - that which some call "dreams" - you know them of Spirit - that they are not dreams - - call them plays if you will - yet they are none of these things - they are experiences however in Spirit - Spirit speaketh and Spirit heareth and responds -- While it is not as one might <u>think</u> - it is never-the-less of Spirit --

The work which we are to do shall be that of Spirit - not of flesh -- Yet it is not necessary that you be in the world of Spirit - as it is called you are to do a great work while in flesh - - yet thy work shall be of - thru - and of Spirit - for all thy inspiration and the Great Revelations shall be in Spirit - - for is not the Spirit Greater - more powerful than the flesh? It is the Spirit that is Lord - and Master of flesh - is it not!

While you shall do a Mighty Work while in flesh - the Greater part shall be done in Spirit -- And for this is it said: "Be ye as one prepared for the Greater Part"- for thou art in school - - now think ye not - that thy schooling is finished - when ye lay aside the coat of flesh - for it is not so!! it simply is not so!! That is one of the fallacies which hast been given thru the churches which we have known-- It is not true that the putting off of flesh makes the man pure or saintly -- Yet - how many times have you heard it said: "He has gone to his eternal rest" --

Well - so much for that -- Now let us speak of the new part which shall be given us - with greater understanding --

We have been shown part of the plan as it is - and that which now concerns us today -- we ask not for tomorrow -- We do that which concerns the Plan <u>Now</u> - - this is as we have been shown --

We go out amongst men of Earth - and We touch and quicken them and we shall speak unto them - that which Spirit gives unto us - as the hour demands - as the opportunity presents itself - and we shall be unto them Guides - and Advisors as it were - as you might call it -- And as they are prepared - so shall they receive - - they shall be as ones led gently and surely -- and we shall remember at all times the law - and obey it to the letter - for we have remembered the lessons learned - we have not forgotten the consequence of disobedience - THE SORROW which cometh from breaking the law - for one slight infraction thereof So be it we have not been <u>idle</u> - we have not been playing the proverbial harp - no - no - not for one hour have we indulged ourself in any such dreaming - for we have worked for this day --

Yet think ye not - we see it as drudgery - - we go forth with glad hearts - that we are so privileged to serve mankind - for it is our joy - - our reward is <u>their</u> <u>freedom</u>-- Praise ye the Name of Him which has made this possible -- So be it ye too shall know - as we - the "Host" knows - for art thou not one of Us by Divine Right - - hast it not been said - that thy passport is in order? It is So -- Fear not! for I say unto thee: Ye are one of the Host - One with the Host - and it is So -- So be it - Amen and Selah --

I say unto thee: I now walk and talk with Our Beloved Master Teacher - and He hast counseled me even as He hast counseled thee - - and I now Know that which I did not know but a few short days before. So be it I am allowed to speak that which must wait - - and ye shall go about the errands of the day - and I shall be with you in Spirit - loving you always - Dad

Recorded by Sister Thedra

THE HORRIBLE DAY FOR PAKISTAN

Sori Sori -- This is the hour that I come to speak of things which are yet to come - and ye shall be as one forewarned - and ye shall be as one prepared -- So let it profit thee --

By the time this reaches them which are yet in darkness - they shall be as ones which have been prepared - for they shall find that the changes which are to come - within the affairs of Earth - are to come in rapid succession - and they shall be as the ones to take note of such changes - for they shall bear witness of such as come in rapid succession --

These changes of which I speak - shall change the nations - the lives of men -- And the ways of men shall be as never before - for they shall be as ones placed in new positions - strange and compromising -- They shall wonder at their positions in which they find themselves - and they shall rebel - - yet they shall Know they have put themselves in such positions - by their own doing -- And they shall find that they have slept while the enemy hast been about his nefarious business -- So be it and Selah -- Hast he not been at his place of business?

While I say - We are at our place prepared to assist - they give unto Us no credit for being that which we are -- They turn and pay homage unto the enemy - they call him "clever"- wise - and "progressive"-- They pay him his due - and bow before him in adoration - while he takes from them their puny penny - and life substance -- He puts his hand unto their mouth - and puts before their eyes the tinsel which blinds them - and they trip themself over his feet - and see not that which he does -- They are blind unto that which he does - for they have the will to follow the way of the deceiver - he - the enemy --

This I would say unto them: They have been forewarned - and they have not heeded that which hast been said - - they have gone head-long head on - into the trap which he hast laid for them - - now they shall cry: "Help!"

Yet I ask them: "Unto whom cryest thou? Unto whom turnest thou? Which way hast thou taken? Which way hast thou chosen?"--"What hast happened? Why art thou so entrapt? think ye that thou escape the fowler's snare - when ye follow him?" I say: Ye have followed him willingly -- Be ye as one on whose shoulders rests the blame --

For it is said that ye shall be as ones responsible for thine own self and ye shall prove unto thyself that thy strength is not sufficient - that ye need the help which WE are now prepared to give unto thee -- Yet - it is said: Turn from the way of darkness before it is too late --

Wherein hast he the enemy - warned thee to turn back - for destruction lies ahead? - Yet it is So - for he leads thee to destruction - I say: His way is the way of destruction! Pity! is he which follow him the enemy! --

They do not serve the Light with one hand - and darkness with the other - they do not walk the "path" of Light with one foot - and the path of darkness with the other - they are not divided within themself - "They are either with ME or against ME"— Thus saith The Lord --

Now it is come when they shall find that they have filled their cup from his pitcher - and it hast been a bitter potion -- They shall drink thereof unto the last bitter dreg - and they shall be as ones bloated - and they shall writhe in agony - for their bellies shall be swollen - and they shall cry out for relief -- They shall cry long and loud - and they shall find that they have betrayed themself --

Wherein is it said: The way of the traitor is hard -- HARD INDEED it is! Therefore it is said: "Betray not thyself - neither thy trust"-- So be it they have not listened - they have gone head-long into the enemies' "camp"--

There is the pity - they have not listened - they have not heeded! By the time they have found these Mine Words - they shall be as ones in the "Camp" of the enemy - and they shall know they have been entrapt.

Yet they have been warned aforehand - for it hast been said many times - many ways: "Beware! Beware!"- - that he - the deceiver lies in wait - that he - the deceiver - prepares a table before thee - and places thereupon the portions to tempt thee -- Shall I name them - that ye might be reminded? Why need I name them herein? Hast thou not found them unto thy liking? Why? Hast thou not been delighted with his banquet - set before thee as tempting morsels?

This is Mine reminder unto thee - for it is said: Ye shall be reminded of thy foolishness - and ye shall suffer the consequence thereof - - so shall it profit thee -- It is said: "A lesson learned - is a lesson earned" - therein is Wisdom -- Yet - it is wise to heed - before the fall --

= The False =

Sori Sori -- Let thine hand be Mine - and record this Mine Word - and it shall be placed with that which is to go into the next part which is now being prepared for them which are to read –

This I would say unto them: "There shall be many which come declaring: 'I am He' - 'I am the Great and Mighty One' - 'I am He which is sent of Buddah'- 'I am one sent of Allah' - of God - of him which is called thus and so"-- None - no not one - shall come saying "I am sent of the deceiver"- none shall say: "I am He - which is sent of the Deceiver - to deceive thee? --

Yet I say unto thee: Be ye aware of him which comes saying: "I am He" - test him - I say: "TEST HIM"- Know ye him for that which he is! and ye shall find him either true- or - false --

There is no law which says: "Ye have to follow Me" - yet it is said: "Choose ye this day which way ye go" -- Now ye shall choose - - thy choice is thine - thine alone - - and none shall stay thee - for the choice is wholly thine -- By thine choice only shall ye follow Me - or - the deceiver - How-be-it ye have been as one following him - the deceiver now it is come when ye shall try Me - and Mine Way -- Ye shall be as one on whose shoulder I place Mine hand - and say: "Come"- yet ye shall come of thine own accord - and by thine own will --

Ye shall pick up thy feet - and walk ye forth unafraid - for have ye not followed the deceiver unto the brink of the pit?

I say - ye have stood on the brink of destruction - while I have cried aloud: "Come - follow ye Me - and I shall lead thee into paths of Righteous-ness" - and ye have halted - ye have questioned Mine Authority - Mine Word -- Mine messengers thou hast ridiculed - and persecuted - and wherein hast thou given unto them aid - and comfort? I ask of thee: Wherein hast thou given unto them aid - and comfort? Think ye they art not sent of Me? I say: I send Mine prophets before Me - - Mine messengers - go before Me that ye be prepared to receive ME - and of

ME -- Wherein hast thou prepared thyself for to receive Me - and of Me - - in whom hast thou put thy faith - wherein hast thou found Me wanting? Hast thou tested ME? Hast thou tried Mine Way?

Now ye shall be as one tried and tested -- Ye shall be as one which shall prove unto ME thine worth -- Ye shall be as one on whose shoulder I place the responsibility of choosing thy own way - and none shall be responsible for thee - for it is said: "PREPARE THYSELF for to receive Me - and of Me"-- The Law is set before thee - and it behooves thee to Know that which is written - and said unto thee - for it is by the law - written and unwritten - that ye shall be tried - tested - and proven fit - or- unfit -- It behooves ME to warn thee: "Be not so foolish as to betray thyself - or - thy trust - for there are none so foolish! NONE - I say!"

Be ye as one Called - Know ye Mine Voice - and come ye unto Me and ye shall not be deceived - for I am responsible unto Mine Father for the Word - which is made manifest -- I AM THE MANIFESTATION OF THE WORD - I AM THE MANIFESTATION OF HIS WILL -- So be it ye shall find thy own way - and ye shall be glad -- So be it and Selah --

The Way I have set before thee - - the law is clearly written - that All might understand - that even the foolish might comprehend -- Thinkest thou that I overlook the simple minded? I am aware of them - for the simple minded are greater in Mine sight - than the intellectual fool which <u>Thinks</u> himself wise - - for he is but the foolish braggard - and bigot - which knows not the law - neither hast he the will to obey the law - the law of Love - Humility - Grace - and Wisdom - for he goes <u>his</u> way - delighting in his own wisdom - and in his own vain-glory --

And in his own deceit and conceit - he hast denied the Word Ineffable he hast turned from the way in which he hast been brot --

He hast been brot into this Earth - and set upon his course as MAN - therefore he hast the responsibility unto himself as man - to walk as Man -- While he hast fallen many times - he is now - once again - walking the way of flesh - as man in flesh - for the purpose of bringing himself into the Light of his own Godhood - from beast-hood unto God-hood - for he hast traversed the way of darkness -- Now in this DAY - he shall pick up his feet - and put forth his own effort - and he shall be as one prepared to receive Me and of Me - and I shall be as one prepared to assist -- And I K<u>no</u>w them which are prepared - for I am not unaware of them which are within the Earth as <u>Man</u> - - I know them - unto the last man -- So be it I know them by name - by number - by color - and by their note - - by their light I know them -- So be it and Selah --

= Individuals, Households, Nations =

Sori Sori -- Mighty is the Hand of God -- Mighty is the Power thereof By the Hand of God shall the works be done-- By the Power of God shall it be done as the Father Wills it-- So be it as He Wills - Amen and Selah --

By the Great and Grand Council shall the Will of God The Father be carried out - and the Host shall go forth as His Hand made manifest unto the Nations of the Earth - unto the peoples of the Nations - and unto the households of the Earth - and unto the peoples of the households --

For are the Nations not made up of the households - and the households made up of the people? Therefore it is said: Each and every one shall be as ones touched - and each shall Know he hast been touched -- So be it and Selah --

While it is come that the Host hast gone out as the Hand of God - it is not as yet apparent unto the NATIONS - that which is being done within the households - neither are the households aware of that which is being done in the individual - with the individual - for each shall be separate - one from the other - each unto his capacity - each unto his capacity to receive - and each in his own tongue -- This is the part of the Host - and it shall go forth fully prepared - and equipt for his part - each unto his own --

This I would have ye know: That there is no place wherein they can not enter - no place they can <u>not</u> go - for they are prepared for this day And they which make up the Host - go in Great Strength - as One body, One Man - of great strength - for in Unity there is Strength -- So be it that the <u>One Host</u> - shall be made up of a multitude which are prepared to go forth as a Mighty Army - to do battle against the enemy --

The enemy I say! for it is now come when the deceiver shall no longer hold in bondage the children of Earth - for they shall be as ones enlightened - and they shall no longer be able to say: "We have not been told"--

For this is THE DAY OF REVELATION - when ALL shall be enlightened in the way of the enemy - - and too - in the Way of the Light -- They shall be as ones free to choose their way - and there shall be none sent to bring them out of bondage against their will -- They shall make their own choice - and blame none other for their choice - for they shall be as ones totally responsible for their choice -- The way in which they go shall be theirs by choice - so may it be profitable unto them -- Amen and Selah --

Ponder well that which is said unto thee - for it is so - and may it be of great assistance unto thee - for it is now come when ye shall be as one aware of thy Greater part - - a G<u>reater</u> P<u>a</u>rt - yet not the G<u>reatest</u> part -- For it is as yet not come when ye shall receive the GREATEST PART - for it is said that ye shall do a greater work - that it is not finished - - that ye shall finish thy mission here upon the Earth - <u>then</u> - ye shall know that it is finished - and ye shall receive that which is kept for thee as thine reward -- So be it and Selah --

Fret not for that which is yet <u>un</u>revealed - for it shall be made clear unto thee - as thou art prepared -- So be it I see thee as one which hast within thy hand the power - and the wisdom - to go forward unto the finish - as one Victorious -- So let it be -- Amen - Amen - Amen --

Let it be known that which I say unto thee - for they shall know that I am come unto Mine own -- And they too shall be as ones touched and quickened -- They too shall be made to hear - and know that they have heard -- So be it and Selah --

For this do I say: "Ye shall arise and come forth as ones prepared" and "None enter into Mine abode unprepared" -- I say: Ye shall listen - be at peace - let peace fill thy heart - let thy hand be turned to peace -- Let it suffice that peace is within thee - and ye shall find peace - for no other place shall ye find it --

While it is given unto "them" to look for peace elsewhere - they shall not find it - for peace is not within them - they have not as yet established it within their own heart -- So let them look - and see what they have put within their own closet - let them examine well their own secret closet - wherein they might find that which they have stored long ago -- and that which they have forgotten - or have not cared to remember -- So be it All things shall be brot to memory - brot out and examined - cleaned - forgiven - and forgotten - - forgotten after it is forgiven - - and peace shall reign within them - and nothing shall disturb that peace --

So be it I have spoken - thou hast heard me - and recorded it - that they might know that which I have said -- Let it profit them - and so may it be -- So be it - and Selah --

= Preparation for Each Succeeding Part =

Sori Sori - This is the word I would give unto thee for them which have prepared themself for to receive --

The Way of the Lord is prepared before them - and they have but to walk therein -- Unto these shall be given peace - for they shall not fear - they shall know that their Salvation draweth nigh -- So be it and Selah --

Be ye as one prepared to go before them - that they might have the Word - that they might be prepared -- For hast it not been said: Ye go before Me to prepare the Way for Mine coming - - is it not said that they shall prepare themself to receive Me - and of Me?

They shall be as ones prepared - for it is the Way of the Lord - it is the Way which is before thee -- And ye have found that ye have not <u>as yet</u> prepared thyself - yet - ye shall find that thy preparation is but begun when ye receive of Me - for there is the next part - the Greater part - wherein ye shall receive of the Father thine inheritance - thine Crown -

thine Enua - thine Inheritance in full -- This is the Greater part - this is the part which I call the Greater Part! Put thy hand in Mine - and I shall lead thee - and ye shall attain unto the Greater part - ye shall not fall -- So be it and Selah --

Keep thine hand to the plow - and ye shall not turn back - for it is said: Woe unto him which turns back -- So be it that I bid thee Come - and I shall direct thee -- So be it and Selah --

= Parental Love =

Sori Sori -- Beloved:- Thou hast heard my song - and you have been the one to hear - for you are the one who has responded to my song - the songs which we have known together - which we have sung together - - let this be "our song" - the "Key" unto us -- When you think of me - when I think of you - you will know my Call*- - you will think of the song which you have heard me sing to you of late - and which you have remembered so fondly - for the reason of our companionship of bygone days - when you were <u>certain</u> of my love and protection --

= Others Profit =

It now reminds you of me - therefore it brings us together in sweet fellowship - in loving communion - and for that are we both benefited for know you this: In-as-much as you and me come together in the sweet communion - therein are others to partake of our joy - and to learn from us - as we have learned from others -- So be it we are teachers unto them- even in our unknowing -- Even in a small measure tho it be - it is as the beginning of their learning of Greater things - Greater revelation yet to come -- And have we not seen them eagerly come to see - to watch - and learn - even as I did -- This is the beginning of a Greater Work - a Greater Service - and you and me shall know that Greater Service - and be glad for our part - small as it may have been - or - small as it may have seemed at the time -- It is said: "There are no small parts - no unnecessary parts - all shall fit into one Great Whole - as the Perfect Plan"

Such is the plan which hast been revealed unto us at this time -- Yet I would not have you think that <u>All</u> hast been revealed unto us - for there is yet more to be revealed -- While it is but the beginning of this Great and Mighty Surge of Light - it is not as yet at its fullness - for it is said - that we go forth in Great Strength - yet - with Gentleness and Surety --

We move forward with great strength and surety - oneness of purpose - yet gently - with love and with wisdom - for it is shown us that there is wisdom in this - and purpose - and it is with Great Wisdom that All is not revealed at one time - for it is thot we would be as ones cast down - with our own limitations -- We <u>grow</u> in wisdom and strength - thereby being prepared for greater things - a greater part -- So be it and Selah -- You shall now give unto thyself rest and peace be with thee - and I shall speak again later this day - and you shall put this with the other parts - behind the door yet to be opened -- So be it it too shall be opened unto all which are prepared - for it shall swing wide unto the touch - the TOUCH I say - and unto them which have responded unto the TOUCH of the One Sent -- So be it I shall speak again at a later hour --

*Again Papa drew my attention by singing our theme song

= Rejoicing =

Sori Sori -- This hour let it be said - that the time is now come for many to be brot in - and the day approaches quickly when the Great and Mighty Host shall proclaim a day of rejoicing - when the Sons of God shall sing together as one Choir - in one Grand Concert - and the echo shall reverberate out - and it shall be heard thruout the Cosmos --

It is now come that the ones prepared - shall be brot forth - and they shall be as one with the Host - and they shall be as One - ONE WITH THE HOST -- This I say unto thee: They shall be as ones brot out - and they shall be as ONE with the HOST - and for this shall they rejoice together -- So be it and Selah --

This shall be the Great day - for which they have waited - and it shall be as none other - for it shall be the time foretold - when the Earth shall receive her anointing - - and her anointing shall be as the purification - for she shall be as one delivered of child - and she shall be as the one which hast been purified - and which is now ready to go forth as the Mother of a New Generation - yet to be conceived - yet to be brot forth - - for She - the Earth - shall bring forth a Child which hast not yet been conceived - which shall be as none before --

She shall bear upon Her breast that Child - and it shall Know its Father and Mother - and it shall Glorify the Mother - <u>and</u> <u>Father</u> - for it shall be as the Child of Honor - and it shall wear the Crown of the Sun upon its brow - and none shall take from it its heritage - for its heritage shall be that of Honor and Glory - for it shall be conceived in Love and Wisdom -- So be it I have spoken - - let them which have ears hear that which I have said -- Let them which have heard - take note of that which is said - and remember well Mine Words - for they have cause to remember -- So be it and Selah -- For this would I say unto thee: Ye shall be as one blest to remember - so let it be -- Amen and Selah --

= Silence =

Sori Sori -- For this day let it be said that the Way of the Lord is now prepared before thee -- The time is come - and the hour struck - when ye shall see that which ye have not seen - - for thine eyes shall be unblinded - and ye shall see and KNOW - and ye shall be glad -- So be it and Selah --

Yet it is said: Ye shall neither speak of - nor write that which ye see for it cannot be spoken - or written -- It is for thine own sake that these things are revealed unto thee - that ye be better prepared to lead them out of darkness - - it is for their sake that ye be prepared for to lead them -- So be it and Selah --

= Give with Wisdom =

These which are of a mind to learn as thou hast learned - shall be as ones prepared for such revelations - for it is said: As they are prepared so shall they receive - it is the law -- So be it and Selah -- Give not unto the unprepared that which is meant for the prepared ones - for they would but rend thee -- Give not thine pearls without price - unto the babes which know not their worth - - for it is said: These are thine - take them unto thyself and cherish them - for they are for thyself alone. Make them thy own - and ye shall cherish them as the Gems without price -- So be it and Selah --

Fortune thyself the part prepared for thee - and ye shall stand upon the High Holy Mount - as I stand - and see from afar - as I see - and know as I Know - and do that which I do -- And no man shall stay thee no man shall deter thee - neither thine hand -- So be it I have spoken - thou hast heard Me - and reported that which hast been said - - now ye shall place this within the record - that they might find it as Mine testimony unto thee - and they shall do with it as they will --

Yet it is said: Woe unto him which spits upon Mine Word - neither shall he put his foot upon it - for it is the WORD Immaculate - and it shall not perish from the Earth -- So let it be Known - and hear ye this: I Am Come that ALL men might hear and see - - yet they have not heard or seen -- While it is a Gift endowed unto them of the Father Which hast Sent Me they have not prepared themself - for they have not opened their eyes - neither have they taken their fingers out of their ears - - they come bearing gifts unacceptable unto Me - they make a mockery of Mine Word - for they are filled with conceit - and they are as ones filled with vomit - they are sick - sick I say! They bear malice - and hatred - they are filled with preconceived ideas - and opinions - they think themself prepared - wise - they THINK themself wise --

So be it I cannot reach them - for I see them as ones - for that matter I KNOW them to be as ones wanting -- They are not self-sufficient - they need assistance - - for this am I come - for this have I given unto thee assistance that ye assist them --

Yet they come as ones which have their cup filled with the offal of their own poor mind - their own cropping -- They are not the wise ones they think themself to be -- Give unto these no time - no energy - for they shall go their way and find for themself that they have betrayed themself -- They shall wait the day - the hour - when they can come with the clean empty cup - THEN it shall be filled - even as it is written. And that which is written is written - and it shall stand as VALID - for it is so - so let it be - Amen and Selah --

Now ye shall receive this day - them which shall enter into this Mine House - and they shall be blest to enter - and ye shall give unto them this Mine Word - and it shall profit them to receive it - they shall be as O<u>ne</u>s prepared -- For this have I said unto thee: "See them" - for it hast been said: "Ye shall put thyself into thy place - wherein ye shall do that which I give unto thee: to do"-- Yet - I say ye shall make thyself available unto these two - which cometh this day -- Be ye blest - and ye shall bless them as I bless thee -- So be it and Selah --

= Parts & The Whole =

Sori Sori -- Be ye as the hand of Me made manifest unto them which have not the knowledge of this Mine part - the part which we share --

This our part - is but p<u>ar</u>t of the Whole Plan which is being unreeled before thine eyes - <u>revea</u>led I say -- It is as none other day - "this day" it is the day for which they have waited - - they have called it by many names - such as: the day of: "Atonement" - "Judgement" - "The Coming" - "The end" - "The Great Awakening" - The Great Speaking" and the "Day of Waiting"-- Well - is it not all these? I say: It is all <u>the</u>se and more - for <u>the</u>y know not the fullness of the plan -- The awakening is now begun - not complete - no - not complete! The time of the Great Speaking is come - not finished - no - not finished -- "The Coming" is complete - yet not finished - for many come with Me - and they bear the insignia of <u>The Host</u> -- These shall be amongst thee for a time - - and I am come even as they - yet they are as ones on a Mission - separate from Mine - yet Not separate - for We come with One Mind - One Purpose - and as ONE -- So be it that I am the Host of the Host - I speak for the Host - and the Host speak in Mine Name - for I have given unto each - his part - each unto his own - and according to his preparation -- Each hast his place - his part befitting his place - all parts fitting into the Whole - into the Great and Grand Plan - for all parts are but part of the Whole --

These parts are separate - yet not separate from the Whole -- <u>they are but parts</u> --

Let it be seen as the Whole - not the bits - bit-by-bit-- For this do they become confused and weary --

For this do they become confused! Let them see that there is a Plan and it shall be as the <u>Divine</u> Plan - the Plan with a purpose --

= The Purpose =

To bring Light and Freedom to a weary and sad people - to the world of men -- So be it and Selah -- Let it be as the Father hast Willed it - - for this are WE sent forth -- Amen - Amen and Selah --

= Valid is the Word =

Sori Sori -- Be ye as one made whole - be ye as one made whole - be ye as one made Whole - be ye as one made New - and so be it -- Amen and Selah -- For this have I come - for this have I touched thee -- So be it - and Selah --

Be ye as one which hast been prepared for that which I shall give unto thee to do - and ye shall be blest as I have been blest of Mine Father Which hast Sent Me -- So be it - and Selah --

Be ye as one which hast been prepared to go where I go - for I shall lead thee into fields afar - and ye shall be as one free to go and come - even as I -- So be it - and Selah--

Has it not been said: Ye shall go where I go - and do that which I do - - So let it be - for Mine Word is Valid - and I shall do that which I say I shall do - - for Mine Word shall stand -- So be it and Selah --

Mine hand I have extended - and Mine Word I have spoken - - thou hast taken Mine hand - thou hast accepted Mine Word-- I have led thee and now we shall go as One into the places wherein ye shall find that which ye have not found - and it shall profit thee -- So be it and Selah.

Thou hast not feared - for thou hast been as one prepared to go where I have led thee -- Thou hast walked with surety - and feared nought -- So be it I shall lead thee into Greater fields - wherein ye shall explore Greater Wonders - for I have said: I am with thee - and I shall not forsake thee -- So be it thou art <u>not</u> alone - I am thy Shield and thy Buckler -- So be it I am He which is Sent that ye be brot out of darkness. Amen - and Selah –

* * *

Sor Sori -- Beloved: While it is yet early in the day - let it be the time for our communication - for there is less distraction - and the silence is more profound -- Altho the morning brings with it the stirrings and the thots of the day - the greater part of the disturbance is in the afternoon - when the body begins to weary - tire of the stress put upon it by the pressures from all sides -- Be ye as one prepared to rest thy body in this period - for it shall be a protection for yourself - as well as the others about you--

There should be a time of renewing at that time - and it shall be very beneficial unto each within the household to give unto themself this period of rest - for at that time it is so necessary - for there is danger of being caught up in the mass-mind so to speak - - for it is at that time when each draws on the energy within them - and their area - that which is within their own particular force field -- There is the protection however - wherein you are - for it has been shown you that there is protection - there is a system of renewal - there is a plan of renewal - and it is being carried out -- Yet - it is necessary to coordinate with the system and the plan - as it hast been revealed unto thee - You shall remember that which you have seen - and that which hast been shown you is of no small account - it is not to be considered of <u>no</u> account - for it is for thy own benefit that it is shown you --

However - it behooves me to say: You shall be as one with that which is sent forth for thy renewal - thy recharging -- The energy which is at its low ebb shall be recharged - by being quiet and at peace - relaxed and without strain - in the late afternoon - when so many are using their "reserves" – their "reserves" being at a low - - and many at the breaking point - so to speak -- <u>You</u> can - and will help to anchor that energy - by being at Peace - and quiet - at that time --

It is not a complicated - "wei<u>r</u>d" ceremony - it is simple - and profound -- Simply be at peace - and absorb the energy sent forth thru and by the rays which meet and contact that part of your Earth wherein you are -- Be as one blest to receive this Mine instruction - and make of it no dogma - no creed - no ceremony - - just be at peace - and let nothing disturb thy Peace -- Rest assured that I am with thee - and it shall be well with thee.

Does this go in the book?

Yes - for that is it given --

Add to it your question --

Recorded by Sister Thedra

One Knock

This house is vibrant with expectation - for a baby is to be born to a couple here - within the next few days --

At 6 o'clock this morning - a strong firm Knock came upon the door.

As I turned on the light I thot: "This is It!"- I opened the door - to see no one --

I had returned to bed - before I realized the caller was not one earthbound –

The following is the message He left - for the record --

Recorded by Sister Thedra

= Raphael =

Sori Sori -- This is Mine time with thee - and I have knocked and thou hast heard Me - Thou hast invited Me in - and I am come that ye be as the hand of Me made manifest unto them which hear not the "Knock".

I say - We knock -- We are not unmindful of thy privacy - therefore We come by invitation –

When ye heard the knock - it was like unto thee - a knock in the silence and it was unexpected - different from the touch - which is familiar unto thee --

Yet Mine Call shall be that Knock upon the door -- Once I Knock This shall be Mine announcement - this shall be our call - and ye shall know it for that which it is - and none shall hear it within the place wherein ye are - - there shall be no interruptions when We have our communication - this I assure thee --

This is necessary to understand - that ye be not surprised when the knock is heard -- So be it that I shall be as gentle as the dove - and there shall be no shock -- So be it that I come as the Dove - the Dove of Peace.

While the first announcement hast given thee a shock from thy sleep - it is quite understandable - and ye shall be as one afore-warned and there shall be no reaction - no terror -- So be it that I shall assist in the forthcoming event - - for this I come - that ye be assured - and it shall be well - and there shall be Great joy attend the event -- So be it and Selah --

This is the time of the event - and it is nigh unto the time - therefore there shall be many which draw nigh - to rejoice that it is come - for the one cometh in light - and in love -- Ye shall receive him* - for he shall be as a one sent of the Father - that there be light -- Light attends him - light sustains him - and he hast come as predestined - as ordered by the One which is Over All - and he is one which hast the blessing of the Council upon him -- So be it that I am One which shall attend him and he shall be favored of Me - and by Me - for I shall be unto him the Brother - the Elder Brother - and he shall be blest by this One which shall guide and guard his way -- So be it and Selah -- Be ye blest to receive Me - and to Know Me -- So be it and Selah -- For this shall I come again - and again -- Ye may call Me Raphael --

*The words "him" and "he" refer to Spirit - not sex

* * *

Sori Sori -- By Mine hand shall I lead thee forward - and ye shall not fail - neither shall ye fall --

This I would say unto thee: Ye shall be as one prepared for that which I give unto thee to do - and ye shall have no fear - for <u>I Am with thee</u> --

Ye shall go into the places new and strange unto thee - and ye shall remember that which ye see - and do - and ye shall be as one blest to remember - for it shall be as part of thy preparation for the Greater things which I shall show thee --

There are many Mansions in Mine Father's House - and ye shall find therein many places - <u>many places</u> - many parts - and much to learn and as ye learn ye shall Know - - as ye Know so shall ye do -- as ye do so shall ye enlighten others - for as I give unto thee - so shall ye give unto others -- So be it and Selah --

Now ye shall be as one which goes before them - that the way be prepared for them which come after thee -- Ye shall be as one on whose shoulders rests great responsibility - for ye shall be given Greater responsibility - and ye shall be as one true unto thy trust - unto thyself. So be it and Selah --

There are ones which have asked that they be permitted to speak unto thee - that others might profit thereby - And it is so permitted - for they are as ones on whose head I have placed Mine hand - and they stand approved -- So be it I give unto them passport - that they might come unto thee - and they shall be blest - - they which are present shall be blest - and all shall profit thereby --

So be it I now bring one which hast presented himself - - prepared and ordained is he - ordained of Me the Lord God -- For this do I say unto thee: Accept him in Mine Name - for he and I are One - One of Mind - One of Purpose -- One of the Host is he - One am I - - and in Him the Father - We are One -- For this do We speak with one tongue one language -- So be it ye shall understand him which I bring -- Call him that which ye will - yet ye shall know him as an Elder Brother - for he is that --

* * *

Beloved: This is Mine time to speak - and it is with Great love and with thanksgiving that I speak of things of Spirit - for things of the world are so transient - of a fleeting moment are they - - while the things of Spirit are eternal and lasting --

Mine hand I extend unto thee in greeting - in loving service - that I might assist in thy ascent - in thine sojourn -- While I know the climb to be steep - the way long and tiresome - I say unto you: Weary not of the effort - for the reward is great - and the Glory of it far exceeds thy imagining -- So be it that I have gone to heights beyond thy ken - yet ye too have glimpsed the far fields - and ye have given credit where credit is due - and ye have been glad for the assistance rendered --

So be it that Greater assistance yet shall be given - and ye shall accept in the Name of The Father - the Host - and the Elders which are as ones prepared to go forth as thy hands and feet -- When ye are weary and thy strength insufficient - ye shall call - and We of "The Host" shall hear and respond -- So be it in Wisdom and with Love --

There shall be need of help - and it shall be forth coming - in ways ye know not of -- So be it that I have spoken unto thee at this time - that ye be informed of Mine presence - - and ye shall know Me by the Name which I give unto thee -- Ye shall be blest to know Me - therefore I shall speak again and again -- So be it and Selah --

= The Meeting of the Waters =

Sori Sori -- For this hour let it be said - that We come in love and peace We bring with us a Host which are want to speak - yet they are not as yet prepared - for they are but young at this - and it shall be as the beginning of a long training period for them --

We of the Host - shall be unto them Great strength and assistance - for many come from other Schools - other than that of the Earth -- These are eager to learn of the children of Earth - even as ye of Earth are want to know of them - - even as ye are want to know of the ones of other countries of the Earth - - even having much in common - yet different in environment -- temperment and culture - color - size - and for that matter - ye are different from them - as they are different from thee -- They too - are curious about you even as you are about them - therefore you endeavor to learn of them - they endeavor to learn of you.

= Exchange Students =

There is an exchange of communications - an exchange of ideologies - commerce and art - theology --and there becomes a common bond between the nations - the people -- Wherein is it so strange unto thee - that there should be others in far distant fields - far away - places - which are interested in learning of you - the children of the Earth -- And these have asked permission to come - see - and to learn - even as you would - into some foreign land - go to study them - and their customs - to learn of them - and to assist where and when possible --

This is the point I would have you reckon upon - that which I would have you think upon -- And be ye as one thotful - mindful - of this Mine word - for I shall not repeat it - for it is said: it is recorded - - so let it be - for it is plainly written - that all might bear witness of Mine Word.

These which have come as participants within this meeting (which we shall call: "the meeting of the Waters") - are as ones which are prepared to learn - as well as assist thee in thy learning -- Ye have what is referred to as "Exchange Students" - each learning from each other - each complimenting the other - - so it is with these which now look from afar - these which are given permission to come and see - that they might learn - as ye too shall learn from them -- So be it that ye have had the first lessons* in such communications - - now ye shall have greater lessons - for it is now necessary that ye go forward as one prepared -- This is no small part - yet it is but the beginning - for ye shall go out as one prepared - and ye shall be as one which knows that which ye do --

I say it is no fallacy - neither is it a dream - yet the reality of it shall become common knowledge - for thee -- Yet it is said: Ye shall hold thy tongue - and be as one silent for the most part - for they which would bear thee ill will - should be as ones which would persecute - and ridicule thee -- hast it not been done - hast it not?

It is said: Ye shall be as one prepared to go where I go - - so be it that I am not speaking foolishly - idly - I am not being the fool -- I am speaking of Greater things - things which are new unto thee - and things which are unknown for the most part - unto them which would persecute thee --

Now let it be said that there are NONE so foolish as he which THINKS himself wise -- So be it a truth - and I would remind thee - there are none so sad as the one which betrays his trust - for he but betrays himself --So be it and Selah --

Now - ye shall be blest - and ye shall Know that ye have been blest So be it - and Selah -- Let thine hand be Mine and thy Voice be Mine - and I shall give unto thee a part for them - and they shall accept it or reject it as they will- and it is said: Blest is he which accepts that which is proffered unto him - by the Host of the Host -- So be it that I Am He. So be it - Amen and Selah --

= The Outline of the Play of the Night =

I was taking a young boy and girl to and from school -- We were now on the way home -- they were capering on the way - as playful pups - running in and out of buildings - - in one door - out the other - thru the crowded lobbies - and restaurants --

I had waited and watched - and brot them back to the "street" so many times - I realized I too was lost -- I could not find one familiar landmark -- I grabbed the girl by the shoulder - and slapped her left cheek so hard that her head shook - - this was to sober her -- I went into an office to ask for directions -- Here I found some very serious minded men -- I asked how to get to Chicago - - - When I went back to the door I found the two young ones waiting for my return with the information. They were now ready to be on their way - bearing their part of the responsibility (for their own conduct) -- Scene 2 -

The mother has a child in her arms - it is crying in pain - - I am holding in my hand the wet - stale diaper --

I notice the concern of the men who stand by on the side lines - I place my hand on the stomach of the baby - and watch his reactions - - I wait - wondering where I can put this "dirty diaper"- knowing it must be disposed of --

Now the baby hushes the cry - mother has given it water--

The men now take up a collection of money - and come forward with the intent to help us get to our destination -- I realized they saw us as <u>lost</u> and in need --

I dropt the diaper in a trash can - and we moved on - -

= The Sobering =

Beloved:- This is Mine Word unto thee: Ye shall be reminded of this which I have shown unto thee - for it is now come when ye shall sober them which come unto thee - - for they shall be sobered - ere they go farther - they have been going in and out - going in circles as it were --

= The Slap =

There is little time left - as time goes - for them to be sobered - for they shall be brot up short - and they shall find themself wanting -- they shall then cry - and wail: Lord - Lord we are lost --

This is the lesson I would have thee learn: Teach them with a firm hand - - pity not them which have not the mind to learn - pity them not for they would but lead thee afield - and both should be lost --

Give of thy time unto them which are of serious mind - and them which are of a mind to learn - a will to return home - - They which have gone the way of the dog - let him be -- Yet when he comes unto thee - sober him - - be ye as one blest to sober him -- He too - shall be blest - so be it both shall profit thereby --

= They Both Shall Be Lost =

This I would say unto the lukewarm: There is no pity for them which go headlong - willingly - into the lion's den - into the wolf's den -- I say they shall learn - for it is given unto Me to see them as willful - - let it profit them to learn --

= The "Innocent" =

This I too would say: There are ones crying as little children - which have not the strength - nor the power to do for themself - that which ye can do for them - for they have not the lessons thou hast had - neither the year-experiences -- Put thy hand unto their stomachs - and give unto them the water - which shall be unto them the cure for their ills - - let it profit them to take off their dirty garments and cast them aside - put them away - and return unto their abiding place - clean and refreshed -

I say: Ones stand by ready to assist thee - - So be it and Selah -- Place that which I have shown thee before this - and place them within the book - for it shall profit them to heed that which hast been said herein and they shall take heed - for it is now come when they shall remember well what is said --

= Sheep - Bolt - Stray =

That which I say - is for their own good - for I am not foolish -- I am come that ye be reminded of the <u>time</u> - of the <u>serio</u>us business at hand And it is given unto Me to see them running to and fro - as puppies chasing their tails - they are as ones unmindful of the seriousness of this Mine Work --

They run hither and thither in wonderment - in merriment - in the places wherein they might be seen and heard of men and wherein they might find comfort --

= The Call of the Shepherd =

Yet it is said: Awaken! Awaken! And they know not that they are asleep - they sleep on -- Now it is said: Let them sleep! for I shall know which sleepeth - which are dead -- <u>I shall call them</u> - - feed them which I bring unto thee - place thy hand upon them that they be blest - comforted in Spirit -- Let them cast from them the filth which is theirs Carry not their burdens - carry not their pots!.

= Follow Them not into the Pit =

Let them pick up their feet and come forward - - let them know that they must put forth their own effort - for none shall carry them on their back -- So be it that they shall obey the law - and it is the law that they prepare themself for to return unto their place - which is now prepared for them - and they shall find that they shall be as ones prepared for it the place wherein they shall be put -- So be it and Selah --

= **The Harmonics are Recognized by the Initiate** =

Sori Sori -- Be ye as the hand of Me made manifest unto them which have prepared themself for to receive this part -- And it shall profit them to take it unto themself - and remember that which is said herein -- So be it and Selah --

This I would have them know: There are many gathered into the place wherein they are - at the time of reading these words - - these come into the place of reading - for the purpose of assisting thee in the understanding of such as is now being given unto thee -- These are thy Benefactors - they give unto thee assistance - that ye might know that which is not lawful to put on paper - or to print - for it is the language of the heart - and not of a people - not of time -- It is the "Word Ineffable"- and it is in its purity - for not one word shall be given for the purpose of entertaining thee - or satisfying thy own curiosity -- Each word is given for a purpose - which ye come to understand - and it carries with it a message - even as the Sound of Mine Voice - the Sound of Music - which all are not able to interpret or understand --

These which have come to bear witness of these Mine Words - Know the value of them - they Know the music of them - for they are Mine - and I give unto thee no discord - - I give unto thee No discord!

I speak that ye might Know peace - and harmony - that harmony shall be manifest within thee - - and it is said: "Mine sheep Know Mine Voice"-- It is fortuned unto the Host to Know the harmonics of these

Mine Words - therefore I have put them into the mouth of Mine Priestess - that ye might have them - and it is well that ye take them unto thyself - and remember them - for it is now come when ye shall have cause to remember them --

This too I would say unto thee: Discount nought said within these pages - for I am not so foolish as to make nonsense -- I speak as one sober - and I come that they be sobered - for the time comes swiftly when they shall stand as ones shorn of all their power and glory - and they shall cry for Our assistance --

Yet I say unto thee: It is well to be prepared - for it is given unto Me to see what lies ahead of thee -- And too - it is said: "Be ye as one prepared" - - weary not of the Word - weary not of the warning/ the repetition - for it is said: When thou hast prepared thyself for the Greater part - I shall lead thee on to Higher Ground - and ye shall see and Know that which ye have not Known -- So let it profit thee to follow where I lead thee -- So be it and Selah --

Sori Sori-- By Mine own hand I shall lead thee this day - and I shall put the words into thy mouth - that ye might speak for Me - for I say unto thee: Ye shall speak that which I give unto thee to say --

Ye shall be as one prepared - for it is now come when ye shall be given a part - which shall be as one unlike any other - - it shall be as one unlike any other -- Yet - ye shall have no fear - for I shall be unto thee thy Shield and thy Buckler - and it shall be unto thee thy protection And ye shall stand tall - and be as a pillar of fire - for I say - ye shall not be touched by that which cometh nigh unto thee -- Ye shall burn away all that which is of no worth - and ye shall be as one in mind with Me - and no thing shall be unto thee of evil - for I say it shall not touch thee -- So be it I have spoken - thou hast heard Me -- So be it well -- I Am Sananda -

* * *

Beloved: Ye shall now record that which I shall say unto you - for it shall be for this that I speak -- The book which is now being prepared shall be as the lesser part of thy work - for the Greater part is to follow the lesser shall be complete - and then shall ye begin the Greater part.

= Fear / Panic / Fear =

This is the part which I would have you place within the book - and it shall be of Great assistance unto many - many yet unborn -- I say: "Many yet unborn" - for it is now come when many shall lay aside the garment of flesh unprepared - - they shall be as ones in panic - and they shall be as ones fearful - and it shall be as panic - for they have not prepared themself for the change which they call "death"-- This is the pity of it - they have not been as ones prepared - therefore they are fearful - and for this do they panic - - they panic for fear - they are as ones unprepared -- When it is said: "Fear not" - they have not heeded - they fear for their safety - for their welfare - for their future - for their family - and for themself --

Wherein is it said - there shall be changes? And are they not come are they not now come? I say - they shall come in rapid succession - and they shall bear testimony of Mine words - for I say unto thee: These changes shall come in rapid succession and they shall bear testimony of Mine Word -- Yet - it is said: There is no hiding place - no place wherein they can not be found -- They can not be lost from Me -- So be it I know where to find them - and I Know them by name and by number and by color - and tone - - I Know them for that which they are - and each shall be put into his proper place - for which he is prepared -- Some shall find their way into Mine place of abode - yet some shall find that they have escaped the pit by the skin of their teeth - while others shall go into panic - knowing nothing of Me - neither Mine Works -- Yet it is said: They too shall have assistance in time - Mine time - for I Know the Seasons - I Know when the harvest is ripe -- And it behooves Me to say unto them: Turn unto the Light - turn unto the Light! that ye be prepared -- So be it - and Selah --

Wast it not said that I come that there be Light? So See it - and be ye as one blest to receive Me and <u>of</u> Me - for I Am the Light - the Truth and the Way - - walk ye there - in - and be ye blest -- So let it be --

I Am He which is Sent that it be so -

Responsibility and Accountability

Be ye as the hand of Me - and write that which I give unto thee to write for it shall be placed within this book - and it shall bear witness of Me and the Plan - for it shall be unto th<u>em</u> Great Light - them which accepts it -- They shall be as ones prepared to receive - and they shall remember that which I have caused to be written herein -- So be it and Selah --

This is the hour in which I have touched thee - and thou hast responded unto Mine touch -- Now it is well that ye give unto them this Word --

There is a Plan - and it is unfolding gently before thee - and it is necessary that ye be fore-prepared - that ye might have the fullness of it revealed - - for it is by thy preparation that ye receive the fullness –

There is but one requirement of thee

= Preparation =

Preparation is the only requirement that is asked of thee -- Ye shall obey the law - and therein is the fulfillment of thy preparation --

Ye shall be as one prepared - when ye have complied with the law unto the letter - every jot - and tittle - for it is by and thru the law that ye be brot out of bondage--

I give unto thee the law - I give unto thee of Mineself that ye Know the law - that ye be prepared -- Now it is for thee to abide by it - and apply it unto thyself -- Pass it not unto another - for I say: Ye - shall first apply it unto thyself - - and ye shall examine well thy own self - and be ye as one true unto thy trust -- Forge no legiron for thyself - - be ye as one on whose shoulders rests the responsibility of thy own preparation - for I say: None shall be responsible for thy salvation --

Ye shall bear thy own burdens - do thy own part - and weary not of thine own part - for hast thou not chosen it? Hast thou <u>Not</u> chosen it?

Therefore I say: Choose ye this day which way ye go -- Shall ye follow Me - or shall ye choose the way of the deceiver?

For he hast placed before thee many tempting morsels - that he ensnare thee -- Many hast he ensnared - and many there be which would take thee into the pit with them -- I say: Many which would ridicule

Me, Mine Way - would lead thee into the Pit with them - and they would be none the less for having taken thee - - for hast it not been said: Ye shall choose which way ye go? Hast it not been said: Ye shall be as ones responsible for thine own choice?

Wherein is the blame placed upon another - for thine own misfortunes? Wherein hast it been said: Ye shall be as one prepared? Hast it not been clearly stated that Ye alone are responsible for thine own self - and for thy offspring - until they are of age -- When they have reached the age of accountability - then ye shall no longer be responsible for them -- Yet - it is written - that ye shall be unto them responsible for their bringing up - for their training - their direction - and then ye shall be free of all responsibility of - or for them - for thy part hast been done --

= Paternal Responsibility =

Wait not for another to direct them - for it is thy part to accept them as thine own wards - and with full responsibility for their training - that they too become responsible for themself - and their offspring -- So be it that I Am the One responsible for Mine part - and I ask of thee that ye be responsible for thy part --

Now let it be understood - that I am not come for preachments - I am come that "YE" be prepared for the place wherein ye shall go - and ye shall be glad - for there shall be no confusion when ye follow where I lead thee -- Ye shall find peace - for ye have complied with the law - yet - I say: that ye shall find that the way of the traitor is hard and long It behooves thee to make strait the pathway - and forget not that I have gone before thee - to prepare the way -- Think ye not that I am come for the purpose of entertaining thee - - I am come that ye be brot forth as one prepared to go where I go - for I go unto Mine Father which hast Sent Me forth - your Father which hast given unto thee being -- So let it profit thee to enter into His place of abode with Me - wherein ye might be forever free - FREE - I say!

Thou hast not known freedom - since first ye entered the womb of woman -- Thou hast been in bondage - and ye have forgotten thine heritage - for art thou not fallen - art thou not in <u>dis</u>-grace?

Now I say - Arise! come ye forth as one accountable - as one responsible - and ye shall be as one prepared to enter Mine fold - as one of Mine own - - <u>Then</u> I shall direct thee aright - and ye shall be glad forevermore -- So let it be as Our Father hast Willed -- So let it be - - Amen and Selah --

= To the Recorder =

Ye shall now place that which is written on the foregoing pages - between the Closed Door and the next - which shall be as one which stands Wide - and it shall be the Door thru which they enter into the Inner Kingdom/ the Inner Temple -- And it shall be given unto Me to direct thee - and I shall direct thee into the place wherein ye shall see - and know that which is being done - that which is being accomplished- And ye shall be as one prepared to give unto the ones which are prepared to receive - as ye have received -- First I shall bring thee - for thou hast followed Me - and thou hast been as one prepared - - therefore I shall give unto thee that which I have kept for thee -- So be it and Selah --

Ye shall now close that book - and the next one shall begin the next part - it shall close with the last message - which is designed for them which have heard Mine Voice - - them which have not been prepared - It is given that they alert themself - and come forward as ones responsible - as ones prepared - for I say - I have need of them -- Yet - I use not that which is not a part of Mine Building Material -- It is said: "I Am a builder" - - Am I not? I build unto eternal life - - I Am the Master Builder - I build to the Glory of Mine Father which hast Sent Me --

I offer unto Him no unseeming gifts - no puny - shoddy material - for I Know Mine materials - for they have been tried - tested - and I Know them to be that which is durable - that which shall be to His Glory - -

For this am I Sent - that He be Glorified in the Earth as in Heaven so let it be -- I am He which is Sent that it be So – So - let us begin a New Part -- Unto that end do We go forth - as His Hands made manifest. Amen

Recorded by Sister Thedra

Mission Statement

Give the truth to the world. Let it be received where it will. Many will read the messages. Some will accept the truth, others will read through curiosity, a few will ridicule. Yet to all is the truth given, and to all remains the power of choice.

The hope of the world in these times is in spiritualizing all forms of activity---promoting understanding through love and service. These must be the watchwords if the world is to come into lasting peace. We are trying to influence a world that is going astray and could cause undreamed of suffering. We are trying to overcome the thought of materialists and to bring a spiritual outlook into the earthly life. We need the help of all on earth who can think in spiritual terms. The great battle to be fought now is between the spiritual and the material, between idealism and carnalism. You can help by spreading the word---we are asking that you help because the battle may be long and the victory far away.

Halls of Light is not allied with any sect, denomination, political entity, organization, neither endorses nor opposes any cause. There are no dues for membership. Halls of Light is self-supporting through its own voluntary contributions. Halls of Light has but one purpose: to help through encouragement and understanding...

To contact the publishers or to obtain copies of our other books, please contact us at email: goldtown11@gmail.com

Sananda's Appearance

Be ye as one which hast heard Mine Voice and responded unto it - for I speak that ye hear, and I say that which is wise and prudent.

Let it be known that I, the Lord thy God hast spoken and bear ye witness of Me, for I have made manifest Mineself that ye might know Me - and for this wast these manifestations made.

I say that I have made Mineself manifest that ye might see Me with thine mortal eyes; that ye might bear witness of Me. Yet thine companions saw and believed not; neither did they hear, for they were selfish and unprepared - yet, did I deny them?

I say; I came that they which would might see and hear. I went and came again unto Mine own. So be it that I have found; I have given unto the found that they which know not might know; that they might come to know as thou knowest.

Yet, how many hast turned from Me and persecuted thee for Mine Word. It is said, "Woe unto them which persecute Mine servants." is it not the law which they set into motion?

Yea Mine beloved, I say they bring about their own downfall. So be it that I am a compassionate one, and I would that they know what they do. So be it they shall learn well their lessons. So let it be, for this is the mercy of God, the One which hast sent Me.

So be it. I AM The Wayshower, the Lord thy God

I AM Sananda

About the Late Sister Thedra

Since the later part of the last Century, the Kumara wisdom has begun to reemerge into the world. This process began with the late Sister Thedra, whom Jesus Christ appeared physically to while on her deathbed and spontaneously healed her of cancer while she was in the Yucatan, where she had gone to accept her fate and the will of our Lord Jesus Christ.

That is when something miraculous occurred. Jesus spoke to her saying, "My name is Esu Sananda Kumara" and then sent Thedra down to the Monastery of the Seven Rays in Peru to learn the Kumara wisdom. After five years, Thedra was told to return to the United States where she founded the Association of Sananda and Sanat Kumara at Mt. Shasta in California.

While heading this organization, Thedra channeled many messages from Sananda and taught the Kumara wisdom. He introduced himself to her by his true name, "Sananda Kumara" And it was by his command that Sister Thedra went to Peru but eventually left upon being told that her experience there was complete. She then traveled to Mt. Shasta in California and founded the Association of Sananda and Sanat Kumara. A.S.S.K.

You ask, Is There a difference between Jesus and Sananda? Our Lord's name given at birth by his Father Joseph and his beloved mother Mary was Yeshua, thus being of the house of David and the order of Yoseph, he would be called Yeshua ben Yoseph. The Roman Emperors placed the name of Jesus upon the sir name of Yeshua after the Emperor Justinian adopted Christianity as the official faith of Rome and ordered that the sacred books be compiled upon approval of a specially appointed counsel appointed by the Emperor into a recognizable and uniform work titled "The Bible". Prior to this, there never was a Bible per se.

There existed until the time of the Emperor's edict, a selection of many Sacred texts that were employed in the Sacred Teachings, many of which were copies of what the Greeks had transposed from the original texts in the Libraries of Alexandria which were originally compiled by Alexander the Great, and were destroyed by Julius Caesar, fearing that they might prove dangerous to the rule of a Caesar, an Earthly God.

In addition, it was to keep the knowledge of Alexander's Libraries out of the hands of the Ptolemy's who were said to be descended from his bloodline. At the time, Caesar had no way of knowing that vast portions of the Library were already in the Americas, in the Great Universities of the Inca, and in possession of the Mayans.

Yeshua spent many years in the East after his ascension. The Good Sheppard, upon his appearances to the Apostles after his ascension, told them that he was going to tend to his Father's other sheep; which meant, plainly, that he was continuing upon his sacred journey. As The Ascended One, Yeshua took to himself the name of Sananda, meaning the Christed One, and Sananda was thus embraced forevermore by the Great Solar Brotherhood. To many of you this is all new, to others it will be received as a welcome easing of the wall that has so long separated two sides of the same coin. This is being placed into the ethers and the matrix of thought at this time, as it is the time of The Great Awakening, and the Christos is already emerging into the new consciousness.

Authority to use the name of Sananda was given to Sister Thedra when Jesus, (Sananda), appeared to her in the Yucatan and cured her instantly of the cancer that had taken over her body. Further, he allowed a picture of his countenance to be taken at that time that she might realize the occurrence was more than a dream. Thedra had a large format camera called a 620 that she used to take the picture of Sananda.

Sanada's Message to her by Sister Thedra: "Sori Sori: Mine hand I have placed upon thine head, and I have given unto thee the authority to use Mine name. Give unto them the name Sananda, by which they shall know Me as the Lord thy God - the Son of God, sent that ye be made to know me, the One sent from out The Inner Temple that there be Light in the world of men. Now it is come when ones which have the will to follow Me shall come to know Me by that name which I commanded thee to give unto the world as Mine New name.

There are many that shall call upon the name of Jesus, yet they will deny the new name as they are want to do. Unto thee I give assurance that I am the One sent that there be Light in the world of men. Now let this be understood, that they that deny Mine New Name deny Me by any name. So be it I have appointed thee Mine spokesman; I've given unto thee the power and authority to speak for being that which I AM. And I say unto thee Mine child whom I have called forth and anointed thee with the Holy Spirit, thy name shall be as it is now called, Thedra, that name I spoke unto thee from out the ethers, and thou heard Me and accepted that which I gave unto thee; and wherein have I deceived thee? Wherein have I forgotten thee, or left thee alone?"

I say unto thee: "Mine hand is upon thee and I shall sustain thee and you shall come to know that which I have kept for thee. So be it that I have kept thy reward, and at no time shall it be dissipated or scattered, for it is intact. So let this Mine Word suffice them which question thee - let them question, and I shall bear witness for thee. For do I not know Mine servants from the traitors? Do I not reward Mine servants according unto their works or merits? I speak that they might know that I am mindful of Mine servants, that I am not a poor puny priest who has forgotten his servants.

"I say unto them: Mine servants shall be glorified above the crowned heads of the nations which have set themselves apart, and denied Me Mine part of Mine word for they have turned from Me in their conceit and forgetfulness. Now let this go on record as Mine Word, and I shall give unto them proof, which are of a mind to follow Me.

So be it as I have spoken and I am not finished; I shall speak again and again, and I shall rise Mine Voice against them which set foot against Mine servants, and they shall be as ones cast out. So let them ask of Me and I shall enlighten them. So be it I know whereof I speak. Be ye as ones blest to accept Me and know Me for that which I AM." On Saturday, June 13, 1992, at exactly 10.00 PM, at the age of 92, Sister Thedra made her final transition from the comfort of her own bed. When the time arrived, she simply took one small breath and slipped quietly away, without pomp or fanfare.

She left as she had lived: as a humble servant for the greater good. The messages included were given to Sister Thedra shortly before her transition. They are compiled here to give you some idea of the significance of her passing and of the expansion of the work, as she is now free of the physical limitations and the pain of the past. Her work now in the higher realms will simply be an extension of that work.

Divine Explanations

Part - I

The following explanations and definitions of terms used by Sananda (Jesus) and the various Sibors were given by Sananda through direct revelation. They are not alphabetical. These explanations should be read over and over.

- - - - - - - - - - -

"My Beloved Sibors please give us plainly the definitions of the following words that there may be no error on our part." - Thedra.

THEMSELF? What is the explanation of your terminology of "Themself" – "themselves"?

"I (Sananda) say unto thee mine beloved, they which would be unto thee a vessel, unto thee a sibor, unto thee teacher, are as ones enlightened of the Father, enlightened of the Father for the light is in them.

They know their parts well, they have their memory, they have mastered the elements, they can do all the things which I do and they take unto "themself" no credit for they have overcome self. They are self-less. Now I say unto them: them which work with thee are the Selfless ones. They ask nothing for "themself." Now while this is true they are as one.

They are within the great brotherhood of the Selfless Ones - the Ones clothed in white. They are as the Royal Assembly - and each unto his own, yet each for all and all for one. Now while in thy world, they (of thy world) are <u>selfish</u> and they are not for the whole - they ask for self and I speak of these as the selfish ones. I speak unto them in terms which they shall come to know and therein is wisdom.

I say that they shall be responsible for "themself" and as a world of me I say they shall be responsible for their society; they "themself" have created it. Now I speak unto thee mine beloved, I say "ye shall be responsible for thyself. He shall be responsible for himself. They as a whole shall be responsible for that which they have created, while thou art responsible unto thyself for thine part - and not held accountable for theirs. Be it so."

BELEIS? "Mighty is the word and great the power thereof. I say unto thee this word carries with it the part of surrender. The word is the release of power - that which is sent forth by the one which asks of the Father His blessing. It is the surrender of the self - the complete surrender of the personal will and letting the Father's will be accomplished in all things through thee. <u>So be it</u> the accomplishment, the acceptance of the Father's plan."

SELAH? - "The word carries the Seal of Truth - meaning it is without error - no mistake - it is the verification of Truth - not subject to change.

SIBET? – "The Sibet is one which has offered or presented himself as a candidate for the greater learning and for the greater initiation. He comes as an empty vessel that he may be filled. So be it."

SIBOR? - "I am the Sibor of Sibors." - "The Sibor is one which has been illumined of God the Father. He has returned unto the Father purified. He has gone the Royal Road - which means he has overcome death. He has mastered the lower elements - he controls the elements. He can raise the dead - heal the sick - he can create like unto the Father for he has finished his course and won the victory and returned unto the Father the Victor. So be it."

"I am the Sibor of Sibors. I am the first born of Him which hast sent me. Sananda."

LEGIRONS? - "Beloved - I say unto thee: thy opinions and thy dogmas are not the least of these - neither thy creeds. Be it ever that these are great and heavy ones. Now let it be understood that a leg-iron is something which holds thee bound. It is something which holds thee, it keeps thee fast, wherein progress is not possible. Now that progress be made possible, ye shall cut away the legirons.

Knowest thou these bound by legirons? These are to be pitied, they drag them with them, impeding their progress - and they are as ones bound! They are not free - are they? While they serve their sentence - they are as ones bound - they are bond-men - they are bound men - men bound. Now let me say I too am a "bondsman." I came that they may be free. I say I bring unto thee the law which thou shall obey - unto the letter - then I shall give unto thee that which I have kept for thee. Be ye as one prepared for that.

PREPARATION? Now - preparation - what do you mean by "preparation?" "This my beloved is the part which they shall do - the part of preparation is: cleaning thyself of all the opinions, indoctrinations of man. The cup must be emptied. This is thy part, the becoming the "'little child" unopinionated, unscathed and unmarred with or by their doctrines, creeds and crafts. I say the child is un-indoctrinated and un-opinonated and is the virgin mind – (yet it does not remain so long in this world). While the little child represents the empty cup - the empty vessel, the Virgin Spirit, it is given unto the child to be one which has come from other realms and to have been in many embodiments, many times: yet the symbol of virginity. Wherein is it said there are none innocent among thee?

WHEREIN I AM? - "Now while thou art yet within the world of men - I am within mine Father's realm, the place wherein there is no darkness, wherein ALL things are known. I say wherein ALL things are known, wherein there is No mystery.

And too - I say when thou hast attained unto thy Royal Road, when thou hast become part of the Royal Assembly, thou shall know as I - thou shall be as I - thou shall be brought into the place wherein I am, for I say unto thee this is attainment. This is the day of Attainment, the day of "becoming," the day of thy salvation. Know ye that this is Mine day - the day for which thou hast waited? I say unto thee: "This is the day of fulfillment. This is Mine Day. Mine Day is come ---"

What is meant by "ALL THE LANDS OF THE EARTH?"- "This I mean, all the lands of the Earth. I have said it, I mean it as I have said it and there is no mystery of or to it."

ALL MANKIND? "This is Mine people - Mine children - Mine flock - Mine Church - Mine brethren - Mine congregation unto whom I shall minister. By Mine own hand shall they be fed and led. These have I came to find. Are not all hu-man beings considered "Man kind"? by thine own standards. Yet all men are not of me."

WHAT DO YOU MEAN - "WILL IT SO"? - "There is power in the "WILL" and the power which they use to create their own torment and confusion is misused energy. Yet they will this - they will it so. Now when ye will to serve me ye give unto me thy undivided attention, the whole heart - thy heart - thine ALL. Yet I say that they which doth attempt to serve me with one hand and the dragon with the other has not willed to serve me. They are not of me - they are not of Mine flock. I say they are either with me or against me. I cannot accept the one hand while they reserve the other for the dragon. They are not wholeheartedly mine.

I make no compromises with the dragon. Mine shall come out from them and surrender unto me themself - their all - without reservation. This is willing it so - for they will the Father's will be done in them, through them, by them. They leave no energy that the dragon may use. They use all their energy to serve me. This is mine word unto thee."

WHAT IS DARKNESS? - "Thine Un-Knowing - thy darkness comes from the fall of man - which one was with God the Father perfect which didst have his memory blanked from him when he didst transgress."

MAYAS VEIL? - "The result of such unknowing - the darkness which man has brought upon himself. The part he has created for himself."

WHAT DOES IT MEAN TO <u>BETRAY ONES SELF</u>? - "This is the sad part for first the 'fall' came from his betrayal - and it hast resulted in the fall - in the veil of Maya - the "illusion" and in thy un-knowing - in thy own darkness."

WHAT OF BETRAYING "HIS OWN TRUST"? - "The plan is all inclusive and includes <u>all</u> - yet there are ones unaware of the "plan" - (and they are not as included in this temple as yet) - no personal reference unto the ones within this temple. Now when one becomes aware of his part, he is given the law and it is provided for his own good and he has the law clearly stated, plainly recorded, and he turns his face away - that he may hide from it. He puts his fingers into his ears that he may not hear it. He gives unto his benefactors the bitter cup and he goes his own willful way.

He has betrayed himself for he shall be caught up short of his course. When he has been given a chance - a "part" within the plan and he has committed himself, he has the responsibility given unto him for that "part" and should he be so foolish as to betray his trust he shall be like unto one which has thrown overboard his <u>own</u> life belt - poor foolish ones!"

WISDOM? - What is meant by the word "Wisdom?" - "Wisdom is that which is light, the knowledge of the law and its proper use. The right use of the law - and this Mine children is Mine part. I come that ye may BECOME wise! Wisdom is thy divine gift - not of man, for man of Earth is foolish indeed - and he is nothing save that which the Father has endowed him. All else is of the world of "illusion" which shall pass into nothingness in the Light which I Am."

WHAT IS THE "PEARL OF GREAT PRICE, THE PRICELESS PEARL? - "That which I offer thee - thy freedom, thy salvation from bondage - thine inheritance in full - Mine word which is not purchased with coin - not bought, neither is it sold. It is the wisdom of which I speak. Mine offer unto thee is without price - it is the 'pearl' - "Mine Pearl."

WHY ARE MIS-SPELLED AND GRAMMATICAL ERRORS USED IN THESE SCRIPTS?

"I am not a conformist. I am not concerned with the letters of man for I am He which has come that they be unbound by their fetters. I say unto them which desireth the letter - unto them the letter.

I say unto thee: be ye as ones free from such bondage. I stand ready to free thee from thy bondage. Unto thee I say - give unto the letter no thought. <u>Hear</u> what I <u>say</u> for I shall say it in many ways as becomes me and serves mine purpose. I say I am no stranger in thine midst. While they know me not, I know them. I see them bowing down before the Golden Calf - and they worship at the shrines which they have set up. (Their own standards of education.) They guild them and bring unto them burnt offerings - yet they close me out.

Be ye not so foolish. <u>Be ye not so foolish</u>! I am come that ye might have Light - Wisdom - Freedom which is the Father's will. While the letter changeth and passeth away - and the letter is not the law - the letter is of no consequence other than to cause thee to see the "Word." The word is the power which shall provoke thine mind into action and thy mind shall be free from the letter. See what is meant within the Word, and let thine mind be staid on <u>me</u> - the Light, the Way - Truth and Wisdom."

"I am He which hast come - that ye be free: forever free. I am Sananda - Son of God. Once known as the Nazarine, He which was born of Mary, Ward of Joseph.

Recorded by Thedra

Part - 2

THE WHITE BROTHERHOOD AND THE EMERALD CROSS.

THE MANY QUESTIONS ABOUT THE WHITE BROTHERHOOD AND THE ORDER OF THE EMERALD CROSS MAY BE EXPLAINED IN A FEW SIMPLE WORDS.

ONE HAS TO EARN THE RIGHT TO BECOME A MEMBER - EITHER IN THIS LIFE OR OTHERS BEFORE OR AFTER - NONE ENTER UNPREPARED.

THE WHITE BROTHERHOOD - or - THE ROYAL ASSEMBLY is of the Realms of Light---not of Earth. The Ascended Masters have proven themself in the school of Earth (THE SCHOOL FOR GODS) who have trodden the path of INITIATION - overcome the trials and temptations of the mundane world - who have gained their freedom and ascended as the Lord Jesus Christ (Sananda). They have gone the ROYAL ROAD.

Knowing the path of the Initiate -- and its pitfalls -- and sorrow, they extend a hand in Fellowship - LOVE and WISDOM - NEVER depriving the candidate an opportunity to learn his lessons well -- for this is His salvation -- for this do they proffer their hand, NOT to do our part for us, but rather that we become strong and free by our own strength.

The Royal Assembly or the White Brotherhood have known all of the heartaches, the longing, crucifications, temptations and JOYS of the aspirant -- the candidate -- the Master -- the Sibor -- herein lies their strength, their understanding, their great love for us on the path.

Their love and understanding knows no bounds. They give help when necessary for our progress. They also withhold it wisely - should it deprive us of our lessons. The candidate on the path of initiation shall become self-responsible for all his actions -- all the energy allotted him throughout his whole EARTHLY existence - and make atonement for all his misused energy, for therein is his salvation.

There is no one else which will ever make this atonement for us (the candidate) on the path of unfoldment. While the host of "WHITE BROTHERS" Brothers of LIGHT are ready to assist, the candidate shall (MUST) put forth every effort to overcome all the forces of darkness which would deter his progress and earn for himself his freedom from BONDAGE.

THE EMERALD CROSS

THE EMERALD CROSS is a company – and an order of beings who work within the Brotherhood of MAN - and the Fatherhood of God - for the good of all mankind --- And at the head of this group is one known as MOTHER SARAH, the personification of love -- embodiment of all MOTHERS. That is: the LOVE of God made Manifest - in MOTHERS. The blessed Mother Sarah is the head of this Order of the Emerald Cross. And when one earns the Divine right and privileges to associate themselves with this Order, it is the joy of all the Orders - and Brothers of Light. I speak for the Order - for I am known as Merseda. (As told to Sister Thedra of the Order of the Emerald Cross).

COMANCHE - which is the porter at the door - which doth keep out the unworthy, the unjust, the unclean. The Door Keeper - the one responsible for the Temple Gate.

BITTER CUP - that which you would not like to partake of - that which poisons thee, that which is not good, that which torments thee - that which ye have given unto thy brother to torment him which returns unto thee as a boomerang to torment thee - which ye shall receive multiplied - which has accumulated in its swift flight. I say prepare not for thyself the bitter cup for ye shall drink of the portion which thou doth prepare for thy brother. Be ye not foolish - make it not bitter.

BLEST OF MINE BEING - I have given of Mine self that Mine beloved has being.

BLEST OF MINE PRESENCE - Have I not gone the long way? I have gone out from Mine place of abode that I might bring light unto the Earth that she might be lifted up - that the children thereof might be delivered of all bondage - that they might return unto the place from whence they went out. And have I not come unto thee many times that this be accomplished? Have I not done all which has been given unto me to do? Wherein have I failed thee? Have I not done all that I have come to do? - While it is not as yet finished, I shall not fail. My mission shall be finished ere I return unto Mine abiding place. Shall I not be unto the true and shall I not return the Victor?

GAVE OF HIMSELF - Did I not give of Mine Self - hast thou? Have I not been true unto Mine trust? Have I asked aught for Myself? Have I not done that which I have promised? Have I not given Mine All? Have I not come on a Sacrificial Mission? What more have I to give - other than myself?

PORE - The physical body - vehicle which thou dost use.

INITIATION - Thy preparation for the inner temple. Each step is an initiation. One step at a time - the overcoming of self - the world - the becoming that which I am.

COSMOS - That which is unseen throughout many universes by thy eyes. Great is the expanse of the Father's Kingdom and the total thereof is referred to as "throughout the Cosmos."

LORD'S STRANGE ACT - This I shall reveal in Mine own time.

WALK WHICH WAY THY CROWN TILTS NOT - as a Son of God. Do honor unto thy Father Mother God - and thou shall be as one which has the Royal Raiment upon thine shoulders - and ye shall wear it in honor and with dignity.

WHEN IT SAYS IT IS RECORDED - WHEREIN IS IT RECORDED? - In the secret place - in the eth - and within the inner temple - and wherein thou art are many things recorded - which I do speak of. Ye shall see these recordings when thou doth enter into the secret place of Mine abode. I say ye shall read the records wherein are written the records of all thy travels from the time ye left the Father Mother God until thine return unto him.

WHAT IS MICHAEL'S FLAMING SWORD? - "The "Sword of Truth and justice."

Recorded by Sister Thedra

Other Books by TNT Publishing

Who am I and Why Am I here?

The Significance of Existence

Death and the Incredible Life After

Fear of Death Removed

Paradise Regained

Spiritual Laws Revealed

Unseen Forces

Too Good to Be True

The Truth of Life in the Spirit World

He Who Has Ears

The Great Awakening, Volumes I thru VII

The Great Awakening, Volume VIII,
THE WHITE STAR OF THE EAST

The Great Awakening, Volume IX,
I THE LORD GOD SAY UNTO THEM

The Great Awakening, Volume X,
MINE INTERCOM MESSAGES FROM THE REALMS OF LIGHT

The Great Awakening, Volume XI,
THE BOOK OF THE LORD

The Great Awakening, Volume XII thru XV,
TEMPLE TEACHINGS FROM THE HIGHER REALMS

Transfiguration Volumes I thru Volume VIII

Contact us at

Email: goldtown11@gmail.com

Web: https://www.whoamiandwhyamihere.com/order-online

www.ingramcontent.com/pod-product-compliance
Lightning Source LLC
LaVergne TN
LVHW051554070426
835507LV00021B/2580